REVEREND WILLIAM CARWARDINE AND THE PULLMAN STRIKE OF 1894

The Christian Gospel and Social Justice

REVEREND WILLIAM CARWARDINE AND THE PULLMAN STRIKE OF 1894

The Christian Gospel and Social Justice

Stephen G. Cobb

The Edwin Mellen Press
Lewiston/Queenston/Lampeter

Library of Congress Cataloging-in-Publication Data

Cobb, Stephen G.
  The Rev. William Carwardine and the Pullman strike of 1894 : the
Christian gospel and social justice / Stephen G. Cobb.
    p. cm.
  Includes bibliographical references (p.   ) and index.
  ISBN 0-7734-9508-8
  1. Chicago Strike, 1894. 2. Carwardine, W. H. (William Horace) ,
1855-1929. 3. Church and labor--United States--History--19th
century. 4. Church and social problems--United States-
-History--19th century. I. Title. II. Title: Reverend William
Carwardine and the Pullman strike of 1894.
  HD5325.R12 1894.C5353   1992
  331.89' 282523' 0977311--dc20   92-7603
                                                                           CIP

A CIP catalog record for this book is available
from The British Library.

All rights reserved. For more information contact

The Edwin Mellen Press   The Edwin Mellen Press
P.O. Box 450   Box 67
Lewiston, NY 14092   Queenston, Ontario
USA   CANADA L0S 1L0

              The Edwin Mellen Press, Ltd.
                 Lampeter, Dyfed, Wales
            UNITED KINGDOM SA48 7DY

            Printed in the United States of America

For

Dorothy and Donald Cobb

Parents

Teachers

Examples

Friends

TABLE OF CONTENTS

The late 1800's in the United States were a time of great transition. Of particular concern in this book was the transition in values as manifested in the relations between labor and management. American society was dominated, politically, economically, and socially, by corporate interests. Labor became angry and demanded that its grievances be considered and many reformers picked up its cause. Unfortunately, there were too few reformers heard from the pulpits of America. This was a time when many preachers were too busy weaving "sacred canopies" (to borrow from the title of Peter Berger's classic book) to drop over the status quo, building sacred legitimizers for the interests of corporate America.

William H. Carwardine was an exception. He was one of the early reformers fighting for the workers' cause. There are many important questions raised by this phenomenon. Why were the reforming voices now so vocal? What was the intellectual, social, and economic context which encouraged their protest? What was the value orientation under attack, and what was that of the protesters? Where was the "Church"?

William H. Carwardine was pastor of the Pullman Methodist Episcopal Church, Pullman, Illinois, during the great Pullman strike of 1894. We will be discussing the context within which the strike took place, the predominant values to which it was reacting, the activities of Carwardine, and the rationale for his defense of labor when it was extremely unpopular to do so. We will be discussing the transition of values as manifested in the life and struggle of Carwardine. It will be shown that he drew a good deal of his rationale from the social gospel and Populist movements active in the later 1800's and that he was, among others, an important pivotal figure in the transition from an old value orientation into a new one. It will be shown that, when Carwardine reacted to George Pullman and the Pullman

Company's behavior during the strike, he was not attacking them as isolated cases of abuse, but as manifestation of a larger problem. They were specific examples of injustice, but they were also manifestations of the predominant values of their time which caused the problematic relationship between the employer and the employed in general. Carwardine was attacking the status quo relationship between big business and government from the perspective of a Populist-oriented, perhaps Christian socialist critic desiring a fundamental change.

This book is based upon primary source material, much of which has never before been presented except in my unpublished dissertation. I would like to express my deep appreciation to Mr. Arthur Carwardine, the son of William H. Carwardine, who has made his collected primary source materials and personal knowledge readily available to me. He and his wife have been gracious in opening their Evanston home to me.

Before one can understand Carwardine's position in the transition of values, one must first understand the context of the late 1800's. Therefore the procedure of our discussion will be this: the evolution of laissez faire philosophy in relation to capitalism and the "captains of industry;" labor, the social gospel and Christian socialism, Populism and Carwardine; the "Pullman experiment" as a manifestation of 19th century values; the causes and issues involved in the Pullman strike; Carwardine's role in the strike; Carwardine's post-strike expression of continued concern; and Carwardine's enduring contributions.

ACKNOWLEDGEMENTS

The inspiration for this book came many years ago, while a graduate student at Northwestern University. While sitting in the office of my advisor, Arthur Carwardine appeared, suggesting that his father was an important person, and someone ought to do a history on his life and contributions. He also noted that he had saved much of his father's personal correspondence, newspaper clippings, and other sundry items that might be of help.

Arthur Carwardine is the son of William Carwardine, pastor of the Pullman Methodist Church during the Pullman Strike of 1894, the focus of this book. I would like to thank Mr. and Mrs. Arthur Carwardine for opening their Evanston, Illinois, home to me and making their collected materials, personal reflections, and hospitality available.

I want to thank Dr. Frederick A. Norwood, retired professor of Church History, Garrett Evangelical Theological Seminary and Dr. William V. Trollinger, Jr., Assistant Professor of History, Messiah College, for reading and critiquing the manuscript.

Many thanks also go to Lois De Roos and Pam Snyder for typing and proofing the manuscript, and to Susan Bowlen and Pat Doratzak for additional proofing. Lois, Pam, Susan, and Pat are with Faculty Services at Messiah College. They caught and corrected many errors, and any that remain are mine.

I thank William Carwardine for his fresh, courageous stand on behalf of social justice and applied Christianity. May there be more like him!

Stephen G. Cobb
Grantham, PA
Fall, 1991

Acknowledgement of appreciation for permission to cite from particularly valuable works is made to the following:

Cole, Donald B. **Handbook of American History.** New York: Harcourt, Brace and World, Inc., 1968.

Jones, Peter d'A. **The Christian Socialist Revival 1877 - 1914.** Princeton, N.J.: Princeton University Press, 1976.

Kennedy, Gail (ed.) **Democracy and the Gospel of Wealth.** Boston: D. C. Heath and Co., 1967.

Lindsey, Almont. **The Pullman Strike; the Story of a Unique Experiment and of a Great Labor Upheaval.** Chicago & London: Phoenix Books, University of Chicago Press, 1967. (copyright 1942 by the University of Chicago. All rights reserved. Published 1942. First Phoenix Edition 1964. Third Impression 1967. Printed in the United States of America.)

Special thanks also to:

Carwardine, William H. **The Pullman Strike.** Chicago: Charles H. Kerr and Co., 1894. (new edition 1973, Charles H. Kerr and Co., introduction by Virgil J. Vogel)

Dombrowski, James. **The Early Days of Christian Socialism in America.** New York: Octagon Books, Inc., 1966.

Eitzen, D. Stanley and Maxine Baca Zinn. "The Reagan Domestic Legacy: Greater Inequality and Destabilization," in D. Stanley Eitzen, **Society's Problems: Sources and Consequences.** Boston: Allyn and Bacon, 1989.

Smith, Robert T. Handy and Lefferts A. Loetscher. **American Christianity: an Historical Interpretation With Representative Documents Vol. II: 1820 - 1968.** New York: Charles Scribner's Sons, 1963.

Williams, William Appleman. **The Contours of American History.** Chicago: Quadrangle Books, 1966. (new edition 1989, W. W. Norton & Company, Inc., New York)

INTRODUCTION

Methodist minister William Carwardine, unlike most of his fellow clergy at the turn of the century, stood up to the forces of corporate America and clearly and persistently called for justice and equity for working men and women. This may, in itself, be worthy of historical note. What is particularly striking about the Rev. Carwardine, however, is that he was a Methodist minister in Pullman, Illinois, who shrugged off corporate pressures to speak out against the Pullman Car Company and in behalf of the workers during the bitter and momentous strike of 1894. In the pages which follow, Stephen G. Cobb has rescued this brave minister from undeserved obscurity.

A New York City native and former student at Colgate University and the Peter Cooper Institute, William Carwardine was, in 1882, ordained a minister in the Methodist Episcopal Church. After a few years as a pastor in Kansas, Carwardine went to Garrett Biblical Institute (Evanston, Illinois) for theological training, from whence he graduated in 1889. For most of the rest of his career (he died in 1929) Carwardine served churches in the Chicago area. This included the fateful stint in Pullman during the mid-1890's, where his social thought was forged in the crucible of the great strike of 1894.

Cobb asserts that central to Carwardine's thought was the notion that the teachings of Jesus must be instituted in the social order. As Carwardine saw it, this meant the establishment of a Christian socialism "That was founded on the golden rule and the Sermon on the Mount." For Carwardine, as for other Christian socialists of the time, this would include greater governmental regulation of business, increased opportunity for the people to become active in the political process, and the establishment of a cooperative and equitable relationship between labor and management.

Carwardine was certainly not a revolutionary. He called for ballots, not bullets; he did not seek the establishment of state socialism of, as he put it, "the Marxist variety;" he did not desire the destruction of the free enterprise system. Moreover, and as Cobb pointedly observes, the Methodist minister and his fellow Christian socialists were strong on ideals and weak on specific programs. This said, Cobb also makes quite clear that, the lack of concrete policy proposals notwithstanding, the Rev. William Cardwardine did not (unlike other Protestant clergy with avowed labor sympathies) hesitate to stand up in behalf of the exploited.

In this regard, Cobb provides a detailed story of Carwardine's activities during the Pullman Strike. In contrast with the other cowed ministers of the company town, Carwardine preached against George Pullman, his unwillingness to negotiate with the workers, and his failure to lower rents in the town. Cobb provides a thorough summary and analysis of both Carwardine's most famous sermon against the corporation, and Carwardine's invaluable description, **The Pullman Strike**. Cobb helpfully notes that, in contrast with previous descriptions of Carwardine's role, the Methodist minister originally opposed both the strike and the American Railway Union's sympathetic boycott. However, once the strike began, Carwardine ignored the considerable pressures put on him by the company and wholeheartedly supported the workers.

Cobb concludes his book with a chapter on Carwardine's political involvements after 1894, which included a failed 1904 run for state representative as a Prohibition Party candidate. But the real significance of this book lies in its story of the Rev. William Carwardine and his role in the Pullman Strike. Cobb adds an important local dimension to the account of this monumental labor conflict, as well as bringing into focus a heretofore obscure Christian socialist. Moreover, Cobb's book is an important reminder that laissez-faire capitalism had its religious opponents in industrializing America, even among pastors of small churches in company towns.

William Vance Trollinger, Jr.

Department of History and Political Science

Messiah College.

CHAPTER I

THE VALUE CLUSTERS OF THE LATE 19th CENTURY

When the Rev. William H. Carwardine stood up in his pulpit on May 20, 1894, to preach in defense of the striking Pullman workers, he symbolized the culmination of a long process of adjustment of American culture to the new industrial society of the latter nineteenth century. In the 1880's and 1890's mechanization and expansion of the factory system were rapid and created new and complex labor-management problems. The financial panic in 1893 brought the problems to a head in Pullman, a company town of the Pullman Palace Car Company, as well as in other places. Before one can understand the situation in Pullman one must first understand the context within which it originated. Significant events such as the Pullman strike do not occur within vacuums but within a complex context of interacting values. Too often, in attempting to understand the past, we filter events through current values and thus severely distort situations as they were.

Through the various periods of American history there are identifiable clusters of values which dominated the periods and which manifested themselves in the political, economic, social and religious life of the nation. There is no particular date when one cluster of values suddenly disappears and another begins, but rather a period when simultaneously one declines as another grows. From about 1830 to 1900 a particular cluster of values was dominant in manifesting itself in American life. Because these values were dominant and deep-seeded, deviation from them was interpreted as un-American. However, as the century progressed and industrialization increased, industrialists sought endorsement for the programs they felt were essential to their best interests. They were afraid to abolish cherished American values, so instead they maintained them in "word" but gave them new meanings suitable to their best interests. Thus the cherished American values were still "mouthed" but carried new meanings. It was this re-definition, this distortion of cherished values to which reformers reacted. One must first, however, define the original values before their distortions can be meaningful.

The period from 1830 to 1900 was marked by a belief in linear development, whereby events were seen to have progressed along linear patterns. Related to this belief was another which felt that all of life had a basic wholeness or oneness which rested upon a central essence. History was seen as an organic development stemming from that central essence. For example, when the United States declared its independence, it was felt that from that expression of values a unique destiny was begun which would progressively grow and expand. All of these beliefs, progress by linear pattern, basic wholeness of life, and history as an organic development, were related to the belief that the United States had a uniqueness, a peculiar genius, a destiny formed and directed by God. Out of such thinking came a new, vivid self-consciousness of nationhood, and eventually a dynamic manifestation of laissez faire capitalism. Democracy came to be conceived as the opportunity for self-achievement. The dominant values from about 1830 to 1900 had evolved into laissez faire philosophy. They represented a break from the earlier mercantilist conception of a corporate commonwealth and a new manifestation of laissez faire dogma centering upon free land and the rights of private property, individual competition, and expansion. This evolution to laissez faire philosophy took place as follows.

John William Ward, in his book, *Andrew Jackson - Symbol for an Age*, put his finger on the core of values which blossomed in the 1830's, under the headings of *nature, providence* and *will*. This core of values remained dominant throughout the century, though it received different interpretations as conditions changed.

The values of "nature" involved a shift in mental attitude from that of earlier periods. Influenced by the values of romanticism, emphasis was placed on intuition and common sense rather than systematic thought. Stress was placed on the native strength of the mind and practical common sense, which were seen to have offered power and discrimination of judgment.

The concept of "providence" was also vital to the core of America's uniqueness. Early 19th century America was a time of intense nationalism, when Americans saw themselves as a "latter day chosen race". There was a close correlation seen between the beliefs that God would see to it that America succeeded; that expansion was justified; that democracy was the opportunity for individual achievement; and that history was a gradual organic, progressive, expansive unfolding of the divine plan.

Closely interrelated with "nature" and "providence" was "will". That is, essential to America's uniqueness was the individual's power to will; his self-reliance, determination, energy, and courage. These emphases, nature, providence, and will, were easily modified by rising industrialists to support laissez faire capitalism with its stress on individual competition and expansion, America's territorial expansion, and the definition of democracy as the opportunity for achievement. The American man was seen to have been the master of his own fate, where "the best government was that which governed least."

Since social, economic, political and religious matters are mutually interacting, it is not surprising to find that churches expressed the modified dominant values of the time. William Appleman Williams, in his book, *The Contours of American History*, put it well when he wrote:

According to the Scriptures as well as to Adam Smith's *Wealth of Nations*, therefore, it was moral to pursue one's self-interest because the Hidden Hand would reconcile all conflicts with the general welfare. Competitive free enterprise thus became the master carpenter of a moral community.[1]

Religion thus embraced the task of reforming the moral world so that laissez faire could function in the political, social, and economic spheres . . . and the steady transformation of the abolitionist crusade into an antislavery campaign for free land suggests even more strongly that the underlying element in the situation was the 'Weltanschauung' of laissez faire.[2]

As the century progressed, major units within the nation continued to filter traditional American values through a concept of laissez faire freedom so defined as to favor their personal ability to compete. Of great importance was the type of thinking manifested in such actions as that of Chief Justice Taney, who in 1837 handed down a ruling which sanctioned the corporate form of industrial organization. The corporation was entered among the groups considered to have been legitimate competitive elements within the framework of laissez faire philosophy. Corporations were equated with the individual in the competitive market.

By the 1870's a few very wealthy entrepreneurs, through diverse means of craft and ability, threatened to destroy or seriously limit competition in large areas of the nation's economy. In the tradition of free competition, they cried, "keep the field open." It was clear, however, that free competition had taken on a new meaning. The field was to be kept open so the wealthy few could pursue their own interests. The 1870's saw a new concept of elitism, a new order of merit, a new fraternity of wealth backed by a new concept of American progress. The values of nature, providence, and will had taken on corporate-oriented meanings. They were new wine in old wine skins. As Robert G. McCloskey states in his book, *American Conservatism in the Age of Enterprise*, "classical economies and the concept of organic evolution conspired to change the old doctrine of the moral improvement of man into a theory of material progress."[3]

This transition in the meaning of democracy and progress was reflected in the political thought of the times. There developed a somewhat corrupt alliance between business and politics often called, using Mark Twain's biting words, the "Gilded Age." Businessmen and politicians struck "dirty bargains." Business tended to develop and fatten monopolistic traits, to exercise autocratic control over the lives and destinies of Americans. Explanations as to why such a development took place must not simply emphasize that political leaders were "hirelings" of the business community (though to a large extent, many were), for this inadequately accounts for the acquiescence of the voters in allowing it to happen. Cherished American values had undergone a gradual transition, modified to fit the needs of a new industrial age. Enough Americans had become involved in the new industrialism, and re-socialized by the corporate ideology pervading home, church, classroom, and media, that they consciously or unconsciously internalized and accepted its accompanying modified values.

The values of post Civil War America were outwardly those of the 1830's and 40's, but their meanings had been modified, and their order of precedence had been altered. National attitudes toward democratic ideals such as liberty and individualism had undergone a transition. American democratic ideals had not always been wedded to the concept of economic laissez faire. Post Civil War resistance to government regulation of business was not a mere continuation of a traditional democratic bias. Economic freedom, formerly a subsidiary value in the democratic hierarchy, now assumed the status of an end in itself. The position of economic values became preponderant, from "a primary value" to "the primary value."

American democracy was and is characterized by a hierarchy of values, as illustrated in the opening sentences of the Declaration of Independence. One might argue whether the writers of the Declaration meant to practice what they preached to the degree that their words implied. However, no matter the degree to which they meant to practice their proposals, it is significant that at least the values of their time did not allow as flagrant a discrepancy as did the 1870's. At the time of the Declaration, human or moral freedom was at least expressed as the first concern. Worth of the individual was elevated while the rights of private property were implied to have been subordinate. Economic freedom was seen to have been subordinate to human or moral freedom.

Property rights were certainly firmly established as an article of the democratic creed by the time of the Declaration. However, as Carl Becker stated in his study of the Declaration of Independence, the natural rights philosophy embodied in that document held that beneath all local and temporary diversity, beneath superficial traits and talents that distinguished men and nations, all men were equal in the possession of a common humanity.[4]

By the 1870's, the new business elites looked back on the era of the Declaration and viewed it mainly as a crusade to secure the rights of property. They didn't reject the values embodied in the Declaration, but they modified them and changed their order of precedence. The rise of industrial capitalism in America, with its accompanying interests, scientific advance, Darwinian and Spencerian thought, and urbanization, transfigured the going concept of democracy. Civilization was equated with industrialization while progress was defined as the accumulation of capital and the proliferation of industrial inventions.[5]

The new elites of the Gilded Age were hostile to the promises of popular government. Realizing the inadvisability of declaring such, however, they paid lip service to the catchwords of democracy. The meanings of words were modified, subtle enough to escape general observation. A new content was injected into the traditional terms, and it was generally supposed that nothing had happened since the labels remained unchanged. Gradually, the transitionized values of democracy permeated the ideational marketplace, the schools, churches, work places, and media, and were accepted as the traditional. Property rights were sacred.

It is important to remember that this transition in values was not a sudden phenomenon of the later 1800's. Throughout the 18th and early 19th centuries during the early phases of industrialization, the prestige of property rights had gradually increased. By 1870, under the pressure of the capitalistic ethic, property rights surpassed human rights in the hierarchy of democratic values. This is not to say that human rights were silenced, but in the democratic theory, rights of property took precedence.

Vernon Parrington, in *Main Currents in American Thought*, particularly volume III entitled, *The Beginnings of Critical Realism in America*, dealt with this same transition in values. He spoke of a shift in economic sovereignty, from a landed and mercantile aristocracy to a new race of "captains of industry". In the captains' rise to power, politicians and political parties were willing servants. As Parrington wrote, "science and the machine were the twin instruments for creating a new civilization, of which the technologist and the industrialist were the high priests."[6] This new industrialization required expansion, and the push upon the frontier was great. Expansion and building gave a new importance to the railroad, and so, especially from

1850 to 1869, the "railway age" developed. The "energetic East", with its accumulation of liquid capital, sought new investments in the westward movement. It sought to grow rich, to grasp power, to be strong and masterful and lay the world at its feet.

Having discussed some basic values of the early 19th century, under the headings of nature, providence, and will, it is easy to see how the new industrialism took on these values, with modification, to justify its expansion. The captains of industry, for example, felt the individualism and powerful "will" of their kind was certainly in keeping with traditional democratic individualism. Their individualism undercut, they said, the aristocratic privilege system of decadent Europe. Indeed, in the spirit of democracy, they sought to dispossess the government of its rich holdings. Their argument was, that lands in the possession of the government were idle waste, being untaxed and profitless. In private hands, the same land would be developed, and would thus provide work, pay taxes, support schools, and enrich the community. Preemption meant exploitation, while exploitation meant progress. Such a philosophy fit the simple individualism of the Gilded Age, with its acquisitive instinct. Fitting for a nation with the values of nature, providence, and will, the captains said, America under their leadership would give "a society that for the first time found its opportunities equal to its desires, a youthful society that accounted the world its oyster and wanted no restrictions laid on its will."[7]

Such a value orientation was pervading the country toward the end of the 19th century. Influential persons who held such values let their wills be known to important politicians, who, being sympathetic, responded, quick to turn the government into the "fairy godmother" the influential elite wanted it to be. Political opinion was, therefore, turned into the channel of private enterprise. Those who reaped the greatest benefits were the bankers, promoters, and businessmen. Those who reaped the least were the farmers and the factory workers.

Vernon Parrington, in his work cited earlier, gave a good account of how significant persons of the Gilded Age philosophy were able to bring political forces into harmony with their programs of preemption and exploitation. The situation of the late 1890's, he wrote, was ideal for such a move. Post Civil War America was lacking in political philosophies and was opportunist. The party cleavage between agriculture and industry had been obscured, the logic of party alignment having been destroyed by the struggle over slavery. The Civil War had brought increased centralization, while centralization and the spirit of exploitation exalted the doctrine of manifest destiny (providence). The Civil War and the revolt of Andrew Johnson created a passionate environment and some skilled politicians saw an opportunity to have General Grant easily elected President of the United States. With Grant as President, clever politicians could use his military prestige and lack of political sophistication to shift political power to the interests of capitalism. Captains of industry, and similar minded persons, consciously voted for Republican Congressmen who were expected to cast their votes for huge government appropriations and projects which would insure their prosperity. Politicians responded, holding the "modified traditional" values and the creed of profit philosophy themselves, and saw the greatest good to be the shaping of public policy to promote private interests. After the Civil War, politicians in general saw the duty of the state to help citizens make money and to make the political state a useful instrument for effective exploitation. The logic went something like this: "The public good cannot be served apart from business interests, for business interests are the public good and in serving business the state is serving society."[8] The state was to safeguard the public's opportunity to express those traditional values of nature, providence, and will, filtered, of course, through business colored glasses. The corporate dominated ideational marketplace had done its job!

Parrington detected the fundamental problem of such a political philosophy, a problem that was to be manifested in labor unrest such as the Pullman strike. In a competitive order, the government was forced to make choices. As it gave with one hand, it took away with the other. "And so the persuasive ideal of paternalism in the common interest degenerates in practice into legalized favoritism. Governmental gifts go to the largest investments. Lesser interests are sacrificed to greater interests and Whiggery comes finally to serve the lords of the earth without whose good will the wheels of business will not turn. To him that hath shall be given."[9]

Behind the Gilded Age philosophy of politicians and businessmen, and behind the modification of traditional American values, lay a carefully rationalized economic theory. Henry Carey, a distinguished American economist in the late 19th century, held a "patriotic national economy" position. He felt that resources in private hands would increase the national wealth, and industrialism, made prosperous by protective tariffs, would provide home markets for produce of American producers and would help make the country self-sufficient. John Bates Clark, another leading economist in the Gilded Age, defended laissez faire capitalism. In his book, *The Philosophy of Wealth* (1886), he stated that if open markets and free competition were maintained, the result would be the just distribution of goods that society produced and a steady rise in the standard of living for all who contributed to their production. The rich would grow richer, but so would the poor.

Political and social scientists added to the defense of laissez faire capitalism. William Graham Sumner, professor of political and social science at Yale University, was a leading American disciple of Herbert Spencer. In an essay entitled, "The Concentration of Wealth: its Economic

Justification" (1902), Sumner defended laissez faire capitalism on the basis of this popular hypothesis: "The social order is fixed by laws of nature precisely analogous to those of the physical order. The most that man can do is by his ignorance and conceit to mar the operation of the social laws."[10] Again one can see the application, though modified, of the cherished American values incorporated in nature, providence, and will. Sumner combined cultural determinism and the Spencerian theory of social evolution to the beneficence of capitalism.

Religious leaders also came to the defense of laissez faire capitalism. For example William Lawrence, Episcopal Bishop of Massachusetts, wrote several articles, one being entitled, "The Relation of Wealth to Morals" (1901). In this article, Lawrence drew up moral rationales to defend such captains of industry as Andrew Carnegie. He defended their thesis of the "trusteeship of wealth" on the basis of the Pauline doctrine of the stewardship of wealth. It was God's will that some men obtained great wealth, for in the long run it was only to the men of morality that wealth came. Lawrence wrote: "Material prosperity is helping to make the national character sweeter, more joyous, more unselfish, more Christlike."[11]

Andrew Carnegie was only one of many captains of industry, but his thinking was quite descriptive of their general philosophy. In his book *Triumphant Democracy* (1886), he expressed great optimism concerning the quality of the Gilded Age. The philosophy of the age, he said, enabled America's Republic to thunder past the old nations of the earth which crept on at a snail's pace. Again calling upon the values of nature, providence, and will, he showed how America was destined, on the basis of her laissez faire philosophy, to reach the foremost rank among nations. Material success was a means to social progress and a raise in the standard of living for all. He went on to develop his "Gospel of Wealth," where the men of great wealth were to be the trustees for the common good. If his gospel were followed obediently, in due time it would solve the problems of rich and poor and would finally give peace on earth, good will among men.

The problem of the age, he felt, was the proper administration of wealth. Certainly industrialism had its accompanying thousands of workers in factories, rigid castes, mutual distrust between employer and employee and loss of homogeneity within society. However, these "prices" were small compared to the advantages. Such a system insured the survival of the fittest in every department, and that was good, for talent in organization and management was rare, and would rise to the top in the process of natural selection. These select few would then be trustees of the surplus wealth, to administer the wealth for the common good. Carnegie's elitist philosophy said that "this wealth, passing through the hands of the few, can be made a much more potent force for the elevation of our race than if it had been distributed in small sums to the people themselves."[12] Thus the wealthy trustees were to practice their providential talent and will for the benefit of all.

Such thinking as Carnegie's bred paternalism, which came to be much despised by workers. He set up norms to guide the wealthy in their function as trustees. The duties of the wealthy were to set examples of modest, unostentatious living; provide moderately for the legitimate wants of those dependent on them; and consider all surplus revenues coming to them as trust funds, to be administered, in their judgment, so as to produce the most beneficial results for the community. The trustee was to bring to the service of the poorer brethren his superior wisdom, experience, and ability to administer; to do for them the things they could not do so well. An important principle of the gospel of wealth which left a great deal of room for subjective rationalization, was its recommended moderate provision for legitimate wants. "It were better for mankind that the millions of the rich were thrown into the sea than so spent as to encourage the slothful, the drunken, the unworthy."[13] Drawing upon a distorted meaning of good old American self-reliance and will, emphasis was placed on helping those who desired to help themselves, to assist, but rarely or never to do all. "Neither the individual nor the race is improved by alms-giving. Those worthy of assistance, except in rare cases, seldom require assistance. The really valuable men of the race never do, except in cases of accident or sudden change."[14] The problem was a common one; just who, and on what basis, were persons considered to be "worthy of assistance," or desirous or not of helping themselves? Such subjectivity and paternalism was to cause great anger among the working peoples. Many workers doubted that such "moderate provision for legitimate wants" was an expression of respect for the individual's will. Rather, they saw it as a rationalization by the rich to keep more of the wealth for themselves.

Andrew Carnegie held a view similar to that of George Pullman and others concerning environmentalism and the development of "proper values." They believed that the elite, in attempting to benefit the community, should place within the community's reach ladders on which the aspiring could rise; "parks, and means of recreation, by which men are helped in body and mind; works of art, certain to give pleasure and improve the public taste, and public institutions of various kinds, which will improve the general condition of the people."[15]

As most philosophies of elitism, that of the late 19th century was based upon a type of naturalism. There was a natural law which allowed the wealthy to become stewards, which sanctioned laissez faire economics, which guaranteed progress. Those persons who dissented from this view were indicted much as were dissenters in the past and today through the use of over-generalizations, loaded words, and appeals to American traditional values. As Carnegie himself said, "the *Socialist* or *Anarchist* who seeks to *overturn* present conditions is to be regarded as *attacking* the *foundation* upon which *civilization* itself rests, for civilization took its start from the day that the capable, industrious workman said to his incompetent and lazy fellow, 'If thou dost not sow, thou shalt not reap', and thus ended primitive *Communism* by separating the drones from the bees."[16] (italics mine) As has been done innumerable times, dissenters were lumped into one basket, judged by the established version of democracy and tradition, and were declared to have been un-American and subversive. The "opposition" was made to appear as a challenge to America's unique destiny, essence, progress, and providential greatness. Civilization, said the captains of industry, depended on the sanctity of private property where the laborer had a right to his hundred dollars in the savings bank, but the millionaire had the equal and legal right to his millions of dollars. Clearly, property rights had superseded human rights in the hierarchy of American values.

The era of the captains of industry has sometimes been referred to as the time of splendid audacity and immense wastefulness. Among the chief figures of the period were the "Wall Street Crowd," such as Daniel Drew, Commodore Vanderbilt, Jim Fisk, Jay Gould, and Russell Sage. These men have been characterized by many as blackguards, railway wreckers, cheaters and swindlers. There were also the "Politicians," such as Boss Tweed, Fernando Wood, G. Oakey Hall, Senator Pomeroy, Senator Cameron, and Roscoe Conkling. Again, many critics characterized them as blackguards, looters of city treasuries, and buyers and sellers of legislative votes. Then there were the "Professional Keepers of the Public Morals," such as Anthony Comstock, Dwight L. Moody, Henry Ward Beecher, and T. Dewitt Talmage. They have often been classified as ardent proselytizers, unintellectual, narrow minded, zealous and eloquent. Of course, there were many captains, such as Phil Armour, Nelson Morris, and George Pullman in Chicago; Mark Hanna in Cleveland; John D. Rockefeller in New York; Andrew Carnegie in Pittsburgh; C. C. Washburn and Charles A. Pillsbury in

Minneapolis; and Leland Stanford and Collis P. Huntington in San Francisco. Vernon Parrington looked back upon the time, recognized the distortion of traditional values, and said: "Freedom had become individualism, and individualism had become the inalienable right to preempt, to exploit, to squander. It was an anarchistic world of strong, capable men, selfish, unenlightened, amoral--an excellent example of what human nature will do with undisciplined freedom."[17]

Many men of literature defended and exonerated the Gilded Age laissez faire philosophy. For example, Elbert Hubbard's, *A Message to Garcia* (1899) was an example of success literature so popular during the period, and children, reading the Horatio Alger books, dreamed of the time they might follow in the steps of their heroes. Hubbard's book was printed for mass distribution by many business firms, and perhaps 40 million copies were issued.[18]

The success of the captains and the popularity of their success stories illustrated that their modified American values were widely held. As railroad building boomed between 1868 and 1893, many Americans in all walks of life dreamed of the economic progress that cheap transportation could bring, to merchants, farmers, and whole communities. Enthusiastic persons visualized new industry, new jobs, better markets, and rising property values that canals and railroads would create. They reasoned, that transportation increased efficiency, which stimulated economic growth, which caused new and more production, which reduced the cost of production, which widened the markets, which then created a need for more labor, capital, mass markets, and thus mass production. Particularly important to this rationalization was the rapid growth of the iron and steel industry, stimulated greatly by the railway boom, which together became the foundation of industrial America during the late 19th century.

A very important by-product of industrial growth, which was to be extremely significant in the Pullman strike, was the growing division between management and labor. Samuel P. Hays, in *The Response to Industrialism*, covered this matter in some detail. The rapid growth of the American economy depended on an increasing specialization and division of labor. The former relatively independent "jacks-of-all-trades" gave way to many interdependent individuals skilled in particular economic activities. One of these specializations was the separation of labor and management functions. Specialized managers and specialized wage earners took the place of semi-independent artisans. Manual laborers no longer organized production or sold the finished products. Such a division of responsibilities caused a gap to develop between management and labor, characterized by impersonal detachment. Suspicion between the two became common. Irritation among workers developed when the economy of specialists gave rise to a division even between dominant and subordinate, central and peripheral economic roles.[19]

Much has been written about the competition, speculation, waste, and dishonesty that accompanied laissez faire philosophy and the age of captains of industry. There are volumes written about the dealings of John D. Rockefeller, Andrew Carnegie, Jim Fisk, Jay Gould, Daniel Drew, George Pullman, and others of their kind. It is enough here simply to say that during this time many Americans seemed to believe that natural resources were unlimited, that property values would continuously rise in times of rapid growth. Nearly every property holder to some degree became a speculator, hoping to make a capital gain, to sell something at a cost far above the purchase price. Most Americans possessed a desire to create wealth, and thus sharp competitive practices developed. It was in the midst of this desire for wealth, competition, and speculation that dishonesty and waste was great. Legislatures were bribed, partisan laws were passed.

During this period of competition, waste, and dishonesty, there rose many persons seriously disturbed over the moral ambiguity the new situation created. They saw that American democracy had historically been based, at least to a greater degree than in the late 1800's, on substantial equality. The economy had been dominated by farmers, mechanics, shopkeepers, and small manufacturers. Now, the transition was rapidly bringing to domination an urban and industrial society dominated by captains of industry controlling great corporations. Old cherished values were still mouthed, but their meanings had been modified and distorted. The response was one of moral ambiguity, and was expressed in the arts, literature, politics, economics, religion, and many other areas.

Charles S. Peirce, one of the earliest "pragmatic" American philosophers, was active during this period of time. In an essay entitled, "Evolutionary Love" (1903) he contradicted the view of Bishop Lawrence, mentioned earlier as a defender of laissez faire capitalism. Peirce strongly opposed the Christian law of love to the Spencerian theory of social evolution, the idea that competition was good in that it produced a survival of the fittest. Peirce wrote:

> Here, then, is the issue. The gospel of Christ says that progress comes from every individual merging his individuality in sympathy with his neighbors. On the other side, the conviction of the nineteenth century is that progress takes place by virtue of every individual's striving for himself with all his might and trampling his neighbor under foot whenever he gets a chance to do so. This may accurately be called the Gospel of Greed.[20]

W. J. Ghent, another critic, wrote an article in 1902 entitled, "The Next Step: a Benevolent Feudalism," later in the same year to be expanded into a book entitled, *Our Benevolent Feudalism*. In this book, Ghent drew a parallel between the new industrial order and the hierarchical society of the Middle Ages. The real outcome of the doctrine of stewardship of wealth, he said, was a benevolent feudalism.

Walt Whitman also reacted to the moral ambiguity of the age. In the first preface of *Leaves of Grass* (1855), he had stated that the genius of the United States was in its common people, who forsook greed and cheap finesse to be full-sized men, unconquerable and simple. By 1871, in his *Democratic Vistas*, Whitman had lost his optimistic exuberance, and spoke of the hoggish, cheating, bedbug qualities of the Gilded Age which had to be conquered by a revival of democratic idealism lest the American experiment fail. He saw the "orgy of acquisitive exploitation" to have been a threat to democracy, for it was "cankered, crude, superstitious, and rotten." In a moment of deep doubt he asked: "Is not Democracy of human rights humbug after all - Are these flippant people with hearts of rags and souls of chalk, are these worth preaching for and dying for upon the cross?"[21]

Herman Melville's book, *Moby-Dick*, also expressed the moral ambiguity of the times. Though first published in 1851, it took on special meaning in the 60's, 70's and later. Filled with much symbolism, *Moby-Dick* criticized the age for its obsessive pursuit after objects which ended up consuming the pursuers.

Thorstein Veblen was a theorist in direct opposition to the thought of the Sumner school. He embodied a good deal of the critical approach that characterized the chief personality of this work, William Carwardine. Veblen was an archenemy of the gospel of wealth, as his writing well illustrated. He wrote *The theory of the Leisure Class* in 1899, *The Theory of Business Enterprise* in 1904, and *Absentee Ownership and Business Enterprise in Recent Times* in 1923. He illustrated the feudal character of the "regime" of private ownership and monetary emulation. In his book *Absentee Ownership and Business Enterprise in Recent Times*, especially the chapter entitled, "The Captains of Industry," he set forth his understandings of the "laws of societal evolution," an idea also found in Carwardine. He admitted that Sumner was somewhat right when he spoke of the captains of industry as a necessary consequence of the development of industry. However, Veblen emphasized, they were a *transient* consequence. The evolutionary process continued and caused a division of functions. The captains had sought and contrived means to turn technological resources to new uses and larger efficiency, always hoping for their own gain in turning out a more serviceable product with greater speed. The mechanical industries had grown rapidly and the captains ascended with free competition. As the volume of industry grew, business concerns increased, and the personal contact between employer-owner and workmen tapered into impersonal wage contracts. The captains' functions began to undergo a division of labor and responsibility between the business manager and office worker on one hand, and the technician and industrial worker on the other. Later in the 19th century, as leading industries became "inordinately" productive in terms of what the traffic would bear, production had to be limited. This meant a cut down in the use of machines and labor. Unemployment became a problem. Captains reacted in ways that would benefit their own profit at the expense of the workers. As one critic said, "in the beginning the Captain of Industry set out to do something, and in the end he sat down to do somebody."[22]

Veblen made a vicious attack on the captains and their system. They achieved their position, he said, because:

> The landed interest, the political buccaneers, and the priesthood, yielded him the first place in affairs and in the councils of the nation, civil and political . . . And all the while the illusions of nationalism allowed the underlying population to believe that the common good was bound up with the

business advantage of these captains of solvency, into whose service the national establishment was gradually drawn, more and more unreservedly, until it has become an axiomatic rule that all the powers of government and diplomacy must work together for the benefit of the business interests of the larger sort.[23]

Veblen went on to illustrate the extent of control big business captains had in art, literature, religion, politics, science, education, law, and morals. Nowhere, he said, did the captains rule the affairs of the nation, civil and political, and control the conditions of life, as in "democratic America."

It was in the midst of the modification of cherished values under the illusion of nationalism, and the ambiguous responses to the modification, that reform movements worked, that new values were expressed, that the Pullman strike occurred, and that Carwardine was influenced and in turn reacted. Four important voices of protest during this period, and four that Carwardine expressed, were the voices of labor, the social gospel, Populism, and Christian socialism.

ENDNOTES

[1]William Appleman Williams, *The Contours of American History* (Chicago: Quandrangle Books, 1966), p.232.

[2]*Ibid.*, p.252,253.

[3]Robert Green McCloskey, "Conservatism and Democracy," *Conflict or Consensus*, ed. Allen F. Davis and Harold D. Woodman (Boston: D.C. Heath and Co., 1968), p. 58.

[4]*Ibid.*, p. 55,56.

[5]*Ibid.*, p. 58.

[6]Vernon L. Parrington, "The American Scene," *Democracy and the Gospel of Wealth*, ed. Gail Kennedy (Boston: D.C. Heath and Co., 1967), p.27.

[7]*Ibid.*, p.30.

[8]*Ibid.*, p.37,38.

[9]*Ibid.*, p.39.

[10]Gail Kennedy (ed.), *Democracy and the Gospel of Wealth* (Boston: D.C. Heath and Co., 1967), p.vii.

[11]*Ibid.*

[12]Andrew Carnegie, "Wealth," *North American Review*, (June, 1889).

[13]Andrew Carnegie, "Wealth," *Democracy and the Gospel of Wealth*, p.7.

[14]*Ibid.*, p.8.

[15]*Ibid.*

[16]*Ibid.*, p.3.

[17]Parrington, "The American Scene," *Democracy and the Gospel of Wealth*, p.35,36.

[18]Kennedy (ed.), *Democracy and the Gospel of Wealth*, p.vii.

[19]Samuel P. Hays, "Industrialism Under Way," *Conflict or Consensus*, p.11.

[20]Kennedy (ed)., *Democracy and the Gospel of Wealth*, p. xii.

[1]*Ibid.*, p.vi.

[22]Thorstein Veblen, "The Captain of Industry," *Democracy and the Gospel of Wealth*, p.108.

[23]*Ibid.*

CHAPTER II

THE PULLMAN EXPERIMENT AS A
MANIFESTATION OF 19th CENTURY
VALUE CLUSTERS

While the labor and social gospel movements, Christian socialism, and Populists were criticizing the contemporary industrial scene, the large industrial corporations kept growing, and the urban manufacturing center gained an even more dominant position in the political economy. Having emerged from laissez faire competition, the corporation accepted the traditional premise of private property and the importance of an expanding market place. A new dimension was added, the necessity of planning economic activity. It became increasingly obvious that if the competitive industrial system and the political economy of which it was the core were not extensively planned, controlled, and co-ordinated, competitive tension and strain could cause the system to explode. The ideal institution for doing this planning was seen to have been, against the desires of the Populists, the large corporation. It was to have the responsibility for planning, controlling, and co-ordinating so as to keep the economy running smoothly and profitably.

The recognition for such planning had several roots. One root was the desire of important corporation entrepreneurs to capture as much of the market for themselves as they could. Another root was that the economy did not in fact regulate itself effectively. Competition often proved to be inefficient and wasteful, and created a fear, common among the privileged in American history, that the consequence might be an economic collapse and social revolution. The panic of 1893, which initiated a depression lasting into 1898, was contributive to this fear. The corporation solution was that of planning the economy through a division of labor and bureaucratic control. A few giant firms were formed to consolidate the main elements and processes of the economic system. It is in this context that the planning and building of the company town of Pullman must be considered. It was an attempt, along with assuring a profitable means of production, marketing, and limited competition, to be a model for solutions to industrial problems. It also reflected the dominant values of "nature" and "will," whereas through reliance on native ability, common sense, and the power to will, one could control his environment and help solve problems that would lead to the destiny of greatness that was by providence his.

George M. Pullman was himself a good 19th century businessman and an excellent manifestation of the modified values accompanying his time. He was the type of hero 19th century Americans liked to consider typical, an incarnation of the self-made heroes in Horatio Alger's novels. In his youth he was poor, but through hard work, self-sacrifice, self-reliance and will, he rose to fame and wealth. He was not highly educated nor a great systematic thinker, but he relied on his native talents of common sense and industry. He had come to Chicago in 1855, when it was America's fastest growing city, as a house mover. He played a major role in raising Chicago's buildings and streets in an effort to put them above the water level of Lake Michigan and the Chicago River to solve seepage and drainage problems.

While moving buildings, he became acquainted with a politician/businessman named Benjamin Field, who had acquired the right to run sleeper-cars on the Chicago and Alton and the Galena and Chicago

Union railroads. They formed a partnership to construct and operate sleeping-cars on these lines. Through the application of a clever combination of promotion, innovation, industry, and craft, Pullman dominated the sleeping-car industry. He bought out his partners and incorporated in 1866, and in 1867 he received a charter for the Pullman Palace Car Company, of which he was president and general manager. He expanded into day-coaches and freight-car manufacturing as well as special services, and thus felt a need for another plant. He chose the Calumet region near Chicago for his new plant because it offered cheap land, low taxes, good transportation, and was close to necessary resources.[1]

Pullman's new plant was to be included within the model town of Pullman, Illinois. The model town was to be a manifestation of George Pullman's plan to solve industrial problems. Reflecting America's modified values, he related labor unrest with poverty and poor living conditions, and in turn related poverty and poor living conditions to the lack among workers of such virtues as frugality, industriousness, and temperateness. Being true to laissez faire philosophy, he assumed that one could improve himself by having proper virtues, that only the lazy and improvident needed to be poor. He was an environmentalist and felt that the general solution to industrial workers' problems and social control was to create an environment that would develop within workers middle-class standards. The company town of Pullman, through planned housing, education, recreation, and social activity, was to cultivate such values. George Pullman felt that model community conditions would attract superior workers, boost employee morale and thus production, and would keep workers contented and thereby reduce absenteeism, drinking, the shirking of duties, and the appeal of labor unions. Of course, the town would also be an attraction and advertisement for the company.

And so George Pullman built his model town in 1880 with the idea
that American industry could plan and construct a town capable of solving
the social problems raised by industrialization. In his own mind, he was
employing a business system for public as well as personal goals. He
wanted to prove that industrialization did not have to lead to social
disintegration and the answer lay in the planned order of an industrial
community. He was experimenting with reform. He was manifesting
Andrew Carnegie's concept of trusteeship.

In the *United States Strike Commission's Report on the Chicago Strike
of June-July, 1894,* George Pullman, in his testimony, gave a good theoretical
statement as to the purpose of establishing the company town of Pullman.
Many other persons who gave testimonies, among them Carwardine, said
there were great discrepancies between theory and practice in Pullman.
However, at this point, the concern is the theory. George Pullman testified:

> The object in building Pullman was the establishment of a
> great manufacturing business on the most substantial basis
> possible, recognizing, that the working people are the most
> important element which enters into the successful operations
> of any manufacturing enterprise. We decided to build, in close
> proximity to the shops, homes for workingmen of such
> character and surrounding as would prove so attractive as to
> cause the best class of mechanics to seek that place for
> employment in preference to others. We also desired to
> establish the place on such a basis as would exclude all baneful
> influences, believing that such a policy would result in the
> greatest measure of success from a commercial point of view.
> Accordingly the present location of Pullman was selected.
> That region of the country was then sparsely populated.[2]

There were other reformers, as Pullman liked to think of himself, who spoke of environmentalism. They felt the physical environment influenced character, poor surroundings had harmful and good surroundings beneficial effects. Alfred T. White, a Brooklyn, New York entrepreneur, was such a reformer. White, who in 1879 published a pamphlet entitled, "Improved Dwellings for the Laboring Classes: the Need, and the Way to Meet It on Strict Commercial Principles", called upon "public-spirited" businessmen to act as trustees, to build well planned and solid buildings, to provide clean, well lighted and well ventilated working areas which would improve the workers' characters but still give the employer a "reasonable 7% return" on his investment. White pointed out that the employer should never give "hand outs", for this did not enhance the recipients' characters. Self-help should be encouraged, in the form of mutual responsibility between the employer and the employed. For example, he recommended that the employer provide planned homes for the workers. The residents should pay their rent in advance and with promptness, while following rules for the protection of property and the rights and comforts of others, charging only enough to show a proper profit.[3]

George Pullman was cut out of the same piece of cloth as was White. The problem with their plans was one of relativity. Who determines whether or not the rent brings in a "proper profit"? Who determines when the rights and comforts of others are endangered? Who determines whether or not peculiar conditions such as those of the depression should or should not cause a decrease in the rents? Such decisions were to become problematic in the town of Pullman during the depression of 1893-94, and what was professed to have been a policy of beneficent trusteeship was declared by critics to have been feudalistic exploitation.

Accompanying the thesis that such model towns would enhance the character of the worker and give him comfortable surroundings while it also brought the company a profit was another motive. Through attractive surroundings and the implanting of middle class values, Pullman was implementing a rather silent but potent means of social control. Many interpreted it as a concerted attempt at repression.

George Pullman had set for himself a rate of profit he expected to make from his model town. The expense of creating the reforming community was to be reimbursed through the charging of rents for the homes and public buildings as a profit return rate of 6% on the capital invested. Pullman himself never denied that the town was to be operated on a strictly business-like basis. He had put the company's capital into the town, because in addition to the reforming principle, he expected the town to be a safe investment. He was attempting to illustrate that with a little good old "American creativity," capital could help labor help itself as well as be profitable. He said: "Capital will not invest in sentiment, nor for sentimental considerations for the laboring classes. But let it once be proved that enterprises of this kind are safe and profitable and we shall see great manufacturing corporations developing similar enterprises, and thus a new era will be introduced in the history of labor."[4]

The *Pullman Journal*, which spoke for the company's interests, made no pretensions that George Pullman and his town were simply philanthropic and divorced from the hope of making a good profit. That the workers would personally benefit from the model town was a secondary matter to the primary fact that the town was a business and commercial project. As an article in the *Journal* for January 7, 1983 stated,

> Given a great factory in a town in which all the workmen had neat and tasteful homes, and in which there was not filth and no squalor, where at every turn they were confronted with object lessons as to the advantage of cleanliness and order - given a factory under such surroundings, and it was

Mr. Pullman's idea that it would turn out more work, better work, and be more profitable than one where the opposite conditions existed. That was the beginning and the end of his philanthropy so far as the construction of the town of Pullman was concerned.[5]

Again the *Journal* emphasized that many writers could not get it out of their heads that Pullman was assumed to be some sort of philanthropic enterprise. It stated:

Until this notion is cleared from the mind it is impossible to get any true conception of what the flourishing little town means and what it stands for. It simply means a place where people who work hard for a living and have small incomes may have an opportunity to live better and in more wholesome and elevating surroundings than they do elsewhere, and it stands for an extraordinarily sagacious investment, from a strictly business standpoint, of a very large capital.[6]

The Pullman Company's management was quite open in its admission that nothing was to be given away.

George Pullman also planned for religious unity within his company town, which would be of the nature to satisfy all, emphasizing not the doctrinal but the moral elements of religion. Therefore he had the Green Stone church built, a beautiful structure that was to house this all encompassing religion. The church would add to social control through commonality of belief, but would also, in the spirit of wise investment, bring a profit. The Green Stone church was to be leased to the worshipers. The high rent of the building, however, caused a great deal of criticism among the town's worshippers. There was another problem, however, perhaps deeper, and that was the conviction with which denominational oriented persons clung to doctrinal distinctions. George Pullman's hope for one large church serving the whole community was impractical. A good description of this impracticality, from a critical managerial point of view, was offered by Mrs. Duane Doty. Her husband was editor of the *Pullman Journal* as well as the company's senior town official, historian, civil engineer, and statistician. Mrs. Doty wrote a very glowing report of the town in a book entitled, *The Town of Pullman*, published in 1893. She described the multiplicity of denominational groups which existed in Pullman by 1893, which is important because it illustrated the number of families associated with the "rebel pastors." The only pastors within Pullman that openly sided with the cause of labor were the pastors of the Methodist Episcopal (Carwardine) and the Swedish Methodist Church. Although these two churches were about the same size, Carwardine was the recognized spokesman and leader.

Another importance of the multiplicity of denominations was its illustration of the impracticality of George Pullman's plan of one church for all. Mrs. Doty wrote:

It is a beautiful theory that the people of a small town come together and support one strong union church...But this plan will never work in practice and should never be attempted. Only a few men are broad enough to listen with patience to any but their own preachers. At least that was the experience here.[7]

She spoke of the attempt in Pullman in the spring of 1881 to organize a union church society. A meeting of about fifteen heads of families was called to discuss the matter. The attempt was futile. She wrote:

A few men presented a plan which they thought would meet with favor; it was for all to unite in a union body and get a broadminded evangelical clergyman to care for our church. But to our great surprise the fifteen men present so tenaciously adhered to their five denominations that nothing could be done. With the Methodists nothing could or would do but a Methodist organization; so with the Baptists, Catholics, and Episcopalians, and the three heathen of the party gave up the scheme of a union church as an impossibility. Soon after half a dozen sickly denominational organizations were effected, and for a year or two starved some very worthy ministers, or would have starved them had it not been for outside aid. This course taught a lesson in the strength of denominationalism.[8]

Another quotation from Mrs. Doty's book was important as it illustrated the strengths of the various churches. The "rebel" Methodist churches served about 250 families.

An inquiry in reference to the church preferences of families in Pullman shows that 75 families lean toward the Baptist church; 250 incline in the direction of the Green Stone Presbyterian church; the Methodist Episcopal church can fairly claim 125 families that prefer the Casino building as a place of worship; the Episcopalians, while having no church organization at present, can (May, 1893), no doubt, claim 75 families as preferring that form of church service; the Swedish Methodists claim 125 families, the Elim Swedish Lutherans 100 families, and they have a fine church of their own on 113th street; the Swedish Baptists 50 families, the Holy Rosary church 375 Pullman families, and the congregation have one of the finest brick churches in the country, it being situated on the corner of 113th street and South Park avenue; the German Lutheran 75 families, the German Reformed church 100 families, the Swedish Mission church 125 families, and the

German Catholics 50 families. Ten of these denominations are now provided with ministers and churches.[9]

Carwardine had a very active program going in Pullman. The *Pullman Journal* of June 30, 1894, in the midst of the labor crisis, printed the weekly schedule of the Methodist Episcopal Church's programs. Meeting in the Casino building on Morse avenue in Pullman, the schedule went like this:

Sunday Services:
Preaching	10:30 a.m. and 7:30
Young Men's class	9:30 a.m.
Sabbath school	2:00 p.m.
Junior Epworth League	8:30 p.m.
Adults' class meeting	6:30 p.m.
Epworth League devotional meeting	6:30 p.m.

Tuesday:
Young people's meeting	7:30 p.m.

Wednesday:
General prayer meeting	7:30 p.m.

Having considered the development of late 19th century values and the Pullman experiment as a manifestation of such, let us now consider in more detail the development of Carwardine's value system that caused him to clash with the "Pullman experiment."

ENDNOTES

[1]Stanley Buder, <u>Pullman: an Experiment in Industrial Order and Community Planning 1880-1930</u> (New York: Oxford University Press, 1967), p.8.

[2]<u>United States Strike Commission Report on the Chicago Strike of June-July, 1894</u> (Washington, D.C.: Government Printing Office, 1895), p.529.

[3]Buder, p.40.

[4]<u>Ibid</u>., p.44.

[5]<u>Pullman Journal</u>, January 7, 1893, p.2.

[6]<u>Ibid</u>.

[7]Mrs. Duane Doty, <u>The Town of Pullman: its Growth with Brief Accounts of its Industries</u> (Pullman, Illinois: T.P. Struhsacker, 1893), p.47.

[8]<u>Ibid</u>.

[9]<u>Ibid</u>., p.46.

CHAPTER III

SOURCES OF CARWARDINE'S VALUE ORIENTATION:

-LABOR-

Carwardine drew from and gave to the movements of labor, the social gospel, and Populism. Therefore it is necessary to briefly discuss the aspects of these movements in which he was involved. Several proponents and critics of the laissez faire philosophy of the late 19th century have been discussed. There were many more who helped develop the context within which Carwardine worked. In 1879, for example, Henry George published his *Progress and Poverty*, in which he denounced the great contrast between "monstrous wealth and debasing want". He proposed a "single tax" that would appropriate all increases in the value of land (called the unearned increment) for the benefit of society as a whole. This program of George's won a large following, and single tax groups sprang up in many places. In 1886, George ran for mayor of New York City, and though defeated made a good showing.

Lester Frank Ward, in 1883, published his *Dynamic Sociology*, in which he argued that Darwin's survival of the fittest applied to animals but not to men who were able to manipulate their environment. Unlike William Graham Sumner, Ward interpreted Darwinism to justify government regulation. This theme, government regulation, was to become very important in the thinking of Carwardine.

In 1885, Richard T. Ely and other "rebel economists" organized the American Economic Association and advocated a "New Economics," saying that man could create a new environment through the use of government power.

Adding to the growing theme of government regulation was Edward Bellamy, who in 1888 published his *Looking Backward*, a utopian novel in which the hero looked back from the year 2000 at the 1880's. In the process, Bellamy was attacking Social Darwinism as applied economically, and called for the nationalization of industry for the good of society. Nationalist clubs were organized to support public ownership of utilities and railroads.

In 1890, Jacob Riis wrote *How the Other Half Lives*, in which he presented a shocking picture of the American urban slums. In 1894, Henry Demarest Lloyd, with whom Carwardine was quite close, attacked the Standard Oil Company in a book entitled *Wealth Against Commonwealth*. Of course, Thorstein Veblen's works were circulating at this same time.

Most all of these critics had one motive in common, a motive that found expression in the labor movement, the social gospel, Christian socialism, and Populism. They all felt that property value had been placed above the value of humanity, that though traditional values were mouthed, their meanings were distorted to benefit corporate interests. The industrial revolution had put the workers at the mercy of the capitalist. The employer owned the factory and the expensive machinery in it, while the worker was simply a wage earner in another man's factory. Often the working conditions were poor, wages low, and hours long. There seemed to be no way out for the worker, in a sense, "no exit"! Workers had tried to fight back, but without organization and without allies, could do little. Therefore, movements were begun to speak to the problems of the new industrial age.

The labor movement had been active during the 1860's, 70's, and 80's, but labor unions were still very weak by the 80's and 90's for several reasons. One reason was the lack of homogeneity among labor, where workers were divided along lines of race, color, and national origin, creating exclusive groups to protect their own interests and keep underprivileged groups at a distance. Another reason was that in the 19th century, workers were largely reluctant to abandon the "American dream" of climbing the social scale, of becoming their own master or employer. They were reluctant to abandon the new industrial order and its conditions, which had been presented as a means to eventually fulfill that dream with the proper application of "will," and thus were apathetic toward unions and collective bargaining which were presented, by corporate leaders, as an interference with the providential, natural flow of the political economy. Even leaders such as Terence V. Powderly of the Knights of Labor wanted reforms mainly to open the way for workers to become property owners in the market place, and Samuel Gompers of the American Federation of Labor said workers should accept the system and get as much as possible within it.

The National Labor Union, which had been formed in 1866, and the Knights of Labor, formed in 1869, both frowned upon the use of the strike. They did, however, recognize that the consolidation of industry required the consolidation of labor. The American Federation of Labor, formed in 1881, did not hesitate to encourage the strike and the boycott in collective bargaining, nor did the American Railway Union, organized by Eugene Debs in 1893 and active in the Pullman strike.

Meanwhile the large industrial corporations kept growing while the urban manufacturing centers gained a dominant position in the political economy. Having emerged from laissez faire competition, the corporations accepted the traditional premise of private property and the importance of an expanding market place. It added a new dimension, the necessity of planning national economic activity. It became increasingly clear that the economy had to be extensively planned, controlled, and co-ordinated. The ideal institution for doing this planning, of course, was the large corporation. Government regulation would be artificial and would upset the natural economic flow. Using the same logic as the captains of industry and their trusteeship, the large corporation leadership felt it had a responsibility to keep the economy running smoothly and profitably.

While the corporation planners said they were serving the larger community through their regulations, persons in labor disagreed. They claimed that the real motive of corporation entrepreneurs was to capture as much of the market for themselves as they could, oblivious to the needs of labor. They also claimed that competition had proved to be inefficient and wasteful, and corporation attempts to increase efficiency and maximize profits were usually at the expense of the worker, through lower wages, cheap and dangerous working conditions, and long hours.

There had been labor violence before the 1890's. The Haymarket Square incident in Chicago on May 4, 1886, was a significant event, in that it greatly affected public attitudes which were to carry into later labor disputes, including the Pullman strike. Because of violence, the manner of presenting the conflicts to the public, and the modified values held by most Americans as to America's "essence" and what was defined as subversive, situations such as that of Haymarket Square caused the courts to clamp down on the labor movement, authorities to act more severely, and the American public to withdraw its sympathy.

The year of 1886 had been a tough one for labor, when 610,000 men were out of work due to strikes, lockouts, or shutdowns due to strikes. On May 4, a group of "anarchists" gathered at Haymarket Square in Chicago to demonstrate against police brutalities. Someone threw a bomb which killed a policeman and six other persons. Though the person throwing the bomb was never found, eight "anarchists" were found guilty by a jury and four were hanged. This incident raised great resentment toward the whole labor movement and brought forth many irresponsible charges of anarchism, widespread suspicion, and hostility.

Due to an increasing sense of frustration and "no exit," there was an intensification of labor violence in the 1890's. The year 1892 saw several incidents, foreshadowing social restlessness that was to remain the rest of the decade. In July, 1892, there was a strike of the steelworkers at the Homestead, Pennsylvania works of the Carnegie Steel Company. It had begun as a dispute over wages and reached a climax when the company refused to deal further with the steelworkers' union. Management tried to incapacitate the union and announced it would treat men on an individual basis only. There was a temporary close down of the works. When the workers prepared to resist the importation of strikebreakers, the management hired Pinkerton agents to protect the strikebreakers. A battle ensued between agents and strikers. Probably as many as nine strikers and seven Pinkerton men died. Forty strikers and 20 Pinkertons were shot. The arrival of the state militia brought order, and was timed in such a way so as to end the strike in the company's favor. The battle had lasted about 12 hours.[1]

Later in July, 1892, there was a similar incident of armed warfare between striking miners and strikebreakers at the Coeur d'Alene silver mines in Idaho. Again, troops were sent "in time to save" the situation.

The railroad failures and financial panic of early 1893 added fuel to labor unrest. The slide began, and by mid April, there was a precipitous drop in the stock market. By the summer of 1893 there was a reversal in the state of the national economy, so positive the previous winter. As the *Commercial and Financial Chronicle* stated, in August, 1893, "the month of

August will long remain memorable...in our industrial history. Never before has there been such a sudden and striking cessation of industrial activity."

Before the year was out, there was no section of the country that was exempt from paralysis. Some 500 banks and nearly 16,000 business firms had sunk into bankruptcy. Samuel Gompers of the American Federation of Labor estimated that the number of unemployed in December, 1893, was about 3 million. A full-scale depression set in. The depression reached its worst point when about 20 per cent of the labor force was without work during the winter months of 1893-94. In Chicago alone, for example, over 100,000 men were unemployed, often without homes.[2] In many cities, police stations and other public buildings had to be opened at night in order to provide places of sleep for the jobless. Municipal and private relief agencies were drained trying to provide even the cheapest and simplest kinds of food for thousands who could no longer afford to buy their own. For the nation as a whole, the real income of the population dropped 18 per cent between 1892 and 1894. Large numbers of unemployed went from city to city seeking work. Magazines wrote of these "tramps," but many of those "tramps" were healthy and willing to work, if they could find it.

The depression raised labor unrest and class antagonism to a greater intensity. Several "armies" of unemployed marched on Washington in 1894, looking for jobs and relief. A well known march was led in March, 1894, by an Ohio Populist, Jacob S. Coxey. He believed that the government bore the responsibility for unemployment, and should therefore provide funds and help men find work. He was told he could not have a hearing in Washington. Beginning with 100 men, he left Massillon, Ohio, and by the time he reached Washington, 400 volunteers had joined. When the "army" of 500 reached Washington, the police were unnerved and attacked the marchers with clubs, injuring about 50 people. Coxey and two other leaders were arrested for illegally carrying banners on the Capital ground and walking on the grass. The idea of the march spread, and about 17 industrial armies set out in 1894 from various localities to present petitions.

Thus the 1890's were a time of widespread anxiety and social unrest. There was mounting discontent among the farmers of the country, while the depression continued to cause strikes, violence, and other forms of protests by the unemployed in hundreds of industrial cities. The *Nation*, in 1894, referred to the thousands of workers who marched on Washington demanding jobs as presenting conditions "dangerously near the conditions of things at the time of the French Revolution." The same year, the *New York Herald* justified the use of federal troops to break the Pullman strike in Chicago on the basis that the nation was fighting for its existence.

Such discontent and nervous response gave rise to subversive interpretations of labor unrest. Labor unrest was subversive because it threatened cherished American values, that is, those "modified traditional" values. In the 1890's men who were usually quite sensible talked gloomily of the imminent threat of communism and anarchism. For example, when Governor John P. Altgeld of Illinois pardoned the anarchists unjustly convicted for the Haymarket bombing, Theodore Roosevelt interpreted the governor's actions as a wish to start a "red government of lawlessness and dishonesty as fantastic and vicious as the Paris Commune." Supreme Court Justice Stephen J. Field used a similar argument in finding a recent income tax law unconstitutional in 1895. He justified his decision on the grounds that the times were extremely dangerous. "The present assault upon capital is but the beginning. It will be but the stepping-stone to others, larger and more sweeping, til our political contests will become a war of the poor against the rich; a war constantly growing in intensity and bitterness."[3]

Such statements as these illustrate the redefined values of American democracy, the degree to which the wealthy held policy making in control, the method of dismissing dissent by defining it as unAmerican and subversive, and the extreme tension of the times in which Carwardine worked in Pullman. Carwardine and others were to be lumped by many into the anarchistic basket because of their condemnation of injustice and the distortion of traditional American values and their plea for reform.

-SOCIAL GOSPEL-

The social gospel movement became very vocal during this time of labor unrest. The churches as a whole had not been giving much moral leadership during the industrial crises and laissez faire economy because they were inclined to accept laissez faire philosophy as almost theological orthodoxy. Having accepted the redefined values of democracy, as expressed by nature, providence, and will, for the churches, as some critics have said:

> Laissez-faire economics was the ghost of the Christian doctrine
> of God's personal providence dressed in the ill-fitting clothes
> of eighteenth century scientific law. It taught that there is a
> good Creator who undergirded human relations with beneficent
> principles, and that if only man would avoid interfering with
> these principles everything would work out for the best...On its
> face this seemed convincingly Christian, but in the true spirit
> of the Enlightenment it eliminated the crucial doctrines of the
> Fall and of human sin, doctrines which point to the necessity
> for regulation and restraint.[4]

A new type of thinking rose, often given the name "social gospel." From 1865 to 1880 it was growing, and by the 1890's it was quite active. Over against the extreme individualism of laissez faire economic philosophy, the social gospel expressed a social doctrine of applied Christianity. For example, they gave a new meaning to the "kingdom of God." The kingdom was no longer seen to have been only other-worldly, but as this-worldly, and ethical. The "builders of the kingdom" were to be the community of the ethically earnest. Walter Rauschenbusch, a leading theologian of social Christianity, gave effective formulation to the new conception of the kingdom of God.

The social gospel also placed emphasis on the immanence of God. God was seen to have been not outside of the social process, but within it. This conception, combined with the popular views of evolution, gave rise to an optimistic attitude toward social problems. God was seen to have been in the act of working out his purposes in society. Scholars of the Bible set forth the Old Testament prophets as great ethical leaders, and the "historical Jesus" was cited as an exemplar and reformer. Men such as Shailer Mathews, Josiah Strong, and Washington Gladden were active in emphasizing these new concepts. They challenged the idea that economic life or the law of supply and demand were beyond the scope of Christian ethics. Still influenced to some degree by the individualism and democracy of the times, a man such as Gladden advocated rational self-love, based on the Golden Rule, which, when combined with egoism and altruism, gave a workable social principle.[5]

Proponents of the social gospel urged that the rights of labor be recognized, that the status quo be changed, that the conditions of the lower classes be improved if revolution were to be avoided. They fought for fair wages, and some of them advocated profit sharing by labor. They condemned the concentration of wealth, unrestrained competition, and the laissez faire philosophy as a whole.

In a later chapter, it will become clear how Carwardine, in his activities in Pullman, illustrated his concern for the labor movement and the social gospel. It is significant, that Carwardine's move into the political sphere was also illustrative of the social gospel movement's trend which effectively influenced political progressivism. Carwardine often said that the

Christian church was too far separated from the laboring classes, that its sympathy lay with the richer element. He was heartened by those clergy close to the social gospel who, he felt, began to realize the power of the church if fair treatment were given to all, and if proper attention were given to the biblical doctrine, "love your neighbor as yourself" in both preaching and living. He urged political involvement on the part of the workers. He urged that they be independent in their politics, in that they would act and vote according to the dictates of their own consciences rather than according to the will of their bosses. He cautioned against coalition politics, whereas the workers would be used, not to attain their own goals, but the goals of those who would exploit them. Often he spoke of his "social creed," where he advocated a co-operative commonwealth, municipal ownership, the eight hour day, female and child labor regulations, and many other reforms. Carwardine thought the Populist/Progressive Henry George to have been one of the greatest men of the century. Therefore, it is necessary, before going into the Pullman strike and Carwardine's role in it, to discuss the major tenets of Populism and Progressivism with which he was closely associated.

-POPULISM-

The American people had become accustomed to view politics as primarily the means whereby people could attempt to realize their economic, social, intellectual and religious goals in life. By the 1890's, as pointed out, changing goals had caused a modification in traditional values, and political parties and legislation had become an instrument of industrial growth and its accompanying problems. When many critics of the status quo found the current partisan politics ineffective for their purposes, they sought new methods of political action. The Populist/Progressive programs were a part of this search, as critics sought organization to express their values. There is considerable material written about these movements, with great disagreement, particularly over the intentions, make-up, and accomplishments of the Populists. In spite of the controversy, one thing is clear, the movement had a great impact. No matter how much or little was actually accomplished through legislation, the Populists released a great flow of protest and criticism that permeated American political affairs during and after the 1890's.

The Populist (or People's) Party rose in the midst of the 1892 strikes. It was a coalition party of groups with similar interests, and when it met for organizational purposes, included representatives of the National Alliance, the Northern Alliance, the Knights of Labor, the Prohibitionists, the Greenbackers, and others. At Omaha, Nebraska, in July of 1892, the Populist Party met and nominated James B. Weaver (Iowa) for President and James G. Field (Virginia) for Vice President. The platform adopted included such planks as: a flexible national currency issued only by the government; a subtreasury plan of loans to farmers; an increase in the circulating medium to not less than $50 per capita; free and unlimited coinage of silver at a ratio of 16 to 1; a graduated income tax; government ownership of railroads, telephone, and telegraph; an eight-hour day for labor; immigration restriction; and telegraph; an eight-hour day for labor; immigration restriction, and all land held by railroads and corporations "in excess of their actual needs" to be reclaimed by the government and redistributed. In addition to the platform planks, there were many resolutions, including reforms for the direct election of senators, the initiative and referendum, a single term for President and Vice-President, restriction of "undesirable immigration," improvement of laws against foreign contract, opposition to the use of private police in labor disputes, and others.

Many conservatives of the time, of course, saw these programs as radical. The Supreme Court, as already noted, declared the two per cent income tax unconstitutional in 1895, and government ownership of transportation and communications was thought to be "straight out of the lexicons of socialism."

Of extreme importance, and vital to Carwardine's thinking, was the Populist's conception of the role of government in the national economy. Their platform read: "We believe that the powers of government - in other words, of the people - should be expanded as rapidly and as far as the good sense of an intelligent people and the teachings of experience shall justify, to the end that oppression, injustice, and poverty should eventually cease in the land." The goal was to end poverty and place political power in the hands of the "people." As one modern historian said, looking back, "few Republicans or regular Democrats believed that the federal government was anything more than a benign policeman who kept order at home and peace with foreign nations. After the Populists, government responsibility for the prosperity of the economy would be a more acceptable tenet of democratic social thought."[6]

In their first election experience, the Populists fared quite well. In the presidential election, the Populist candidate, Weaver, received 22 electoral votes (1,029,846) to 277 electoral votes (5,555,426) for Cleveland and 145 electoral votes (5,182,690) for Harrison. The Populists carried Kansas, Colorado, Idaho, Nevada, and did quite well in North Dakota as well as the north-central, Rocky Mountain, and southern states. Populists elected five senators, ten representatives, and three governors.

The Populists resented the defense of America's business dominated society on the basis of distorted traditional values. They attacked, for example, the definition of naturalism which sanctioned corporate corruption. Populists insisted that hard times, starvation, bankruptcies, unemployment, crime, misery, moral degradation, and other problems were not a result of natural development. They were basically unnatural, and mainly the result of "unwise and pernicious" legislation. Populists saw their function to be that of correcting the errors in human legislation. They blamed the predatory nature of current legislation on the fact that it was initiated and underwritten by a small, parasitic minority in the highest places of power. As "Sockless Jerry Simpson" said, "it is a struggle between the robbers and the robbed." Therefore when the Populists sought to enter politics, they did so as a means to control the distribution of wealth, feeling that men could control their society chiefly through harnessing the productive forces in existence through political means. Norman Pollack, in his book, *The Populist Response to Industrial America*, has a valid thesis when he claims that too many historians have emphasized the Populists as being composed chiefly of opportunists, crackpots, anti-Semites, and conspiracy weavers. Many historians have overlooked the real democratic social force Populists perpetuated, through such persons as William Carwardine. Persons such as he accepted industrialism, but condemned the misuse of industrial laissez faire capitalism which impoverished the individual, alienated and degraded him, threatened him with subsistence living, and exploited rather than served him through the machine. Populism indeed was a progressive social force even though it also had its negative elements. Populism was the first modern political movement of practical importance in the United States to insist that the federal government had some responsibility for the common welfare. It was also the first such movement to attack seriously the problems created by industrialism.

Since this discussion deals with Carwardine's values and reform activities as expressed specifically in the Pullman strike and less specifically in the following years, a brief description of state reform movements during the era and the rise of Progressivism which formed the context within which Carwardine functioned follows.

The first "progressive" governor was Robert M. La Follette of Wisconsin, from 1901 to 1906, who inaugurated the "Wisconsin Idea." This idea included opposition to city bosses, a railroad commission, a corrupt practices act, the graduated income tax, and the direct primary. In Iowa, Albert B. Cummins, elected governor in 1901, also fought the bosses, trusts, and railroads. William S. U'Ren in Oregon led the way toward the adoption by that state of the initiative and referendum, the direct primary, and the recall. Southern reform governors such as Jeff Davis of Arkansas, James K. Vardaman of Mississippi, and Hoke Smith of Georgia made appeals for similar causes.

Hiram W. Johnson was elected progressive governor of California in 1910, and Woodrow Wilson was the reform governor of New Jersey from 1911 to 1912 before he was elected president. By the year 1914, many important reforms had been passed in various "progressive influenced" states. Among the political reforms were the Australian secret ballot, first used in Massachusetts in 1888, and used in all the states by 1910; corrupt practices acts; women's suffrage (enacted in 11 states by 1914, though Ohio and Illinois were the only ones east of the Mississippi River); direct primary (Wisconsin, 1903; effective in 13 states by 1912); direct senatorial primary (Oregon, 1904; 29 states by 1909); initiative and referendum to allow the electorate to propose and pass laws directly (Oregon, 1902; 12 states - all west of the Mississippi - by 1912); and the right of the electorate to recall an elected officer from his office (Oregon, 1908; 7 states - all west of the Mississippi - by 1912).

There were also many social and economic reforms, such as the set up of commissions to regulate railroads and monopolies; employers' liability acts (New York, 1910; enacted in 25 states by 1914); workmen's compensation laws (Maryland, 1902; enacted in 38 states by 1917); minimum-wage laws for women and children (Massachusetts, 1912; passed in 8 other states - all west of the Mississippi - by 1914); pensions for mothers with dependent children (Illinois, 1911; 20 states by 1913); maximum-hours laws (Utah law for mines, 1896; Oregon law for women, 1903) and child labor laws.[7]

On January 21, 1911, the National Progressive Republican League, having been founded by Robert M. La Follette and other "insurgents," issued a platform which called for the direct election of United States senators and delegates to national conventions, the initiative, referendum, recall, and other progressive-oriented acts of legislation. The Progressives took several solid stands. Concerning the relationship between government and monopolies, for example, they called for regulation of business. In matters of finance, they called for the protective tariff and government control of the currency. In matters of labor, they called for a curb on the use of injunctions in labor disputes, the abolition of child labor, the institution of a six day week and eight hour day, and workmen's compensation. In political matters, of course, they called for the direct primary, the direct election of senators, state initiative, the referendum and recall.

A word must be said concerning the Social Democratic Party and Eugene V. Debs. Although Carwardine was not a number of this party, he was in contact with Debs and had much to say about him and his ideas. The Social Democratic Party was organized at Indianapolis and nominated Debs, from Indiana, for President and Job Harriman, from California, for Vice President. The party was renamed the Socialist Party in 1901, and has run a presidential candidate in nearly every election after 1900. There were some previous developments that should be considered however, because contemporaries who were ignorant of them, or twisted them, misinterpreted Debs so as to lump him into the subversive, un-American basket. From 1872 to 1900 Socialism developed as an organization in the United States. Marxian Socialists established the First International headquarters in New

York City in 1872. In 1874, they formed the Workingmen's Party, and in 1877 changed the name to the Socialist Labor Party. Between 1890 and 1895 Daniel DeLeon of the Socialist Laborites tried unsuccesfully to get the backing of the Knights of Labor and the American Federation of Labor. In 1900, the Social Democrats under Debs split from the parent party. That Debs' group was seen to have been quite distinct from the Socialist Labor Party in the eyes of the populace, if not in the eyes of historians, is seen in the fact that in the presidential election of 1904, for example, the Socialists received over 400,000 votes to barely 30,000 for the Socialist Labor Party.[8]

Now that the basic views and programs of the labor movement, social gospel movement, and Populist/Progressives have been briefly discussed, enough of Carwardine's thinking should be expressed to show the relationship of his thinking to these movements. Most of the various programs of the movements just discussed were debated and supported by Carwardine, as the chapter on his role in the Pullman strike will illustrate concisely and in detail. However, Carwardine's life before and after the strike illustrated that his social, political, economic awareness and involvement was not limited to the strike, but was part of him constantly. This is significant, as it shows he was not just climbing on the reform wagon for one hot ride. Therefore, a few letters of correspondence, newspaper articles, and other matters covering a period of many years will be discussed, to illustrate the source and breadth of Carwardine's concern.

He had a great respect for, and a mutual social concern with, the well known Populist, Henry Demarest Lloyd. While Carwardine was involved in the Pullman strike, and under a great amount of pressure and criticism, he began to correspond with Lloyd. This correspondence continued until Lloyd's death, and in the process, a mutual respect and sense of common struggle developed between the two men. Before discussing their correspondence, therefore, something should be said about Lloyd's thinking.

Lloyd, like Carwardine and other Populist-oriented reformers, was mainly concerned with the concentration of wealth and power and its consequences, rather than with the personalities or motivations of the powerful as such. For example, Lloyd said of John D. Rockefeller that personal questions were extraneous, because the main point was the simple issue of monopoly and its repercussions. About Andrew Carnegie, Lloyd said that he had no negative feelings against the man as such, but he was one of the best representatives of the American mercenary system of ordering industry so as to pervert it from the distribution of wealth for the benefit of all to making it an instrument of personal aggrandizement and "cannibalistic selfishness."[9]

Lloyd had a definite view of freedom. He felt man was free only when his society encouraged the fullest possible development of his potentiality. At the Populist Party's campaign in Chicago, in 1894, while Carwardine was in Pullman, just south of Chicago, Lloyd declared that the Populist Party was more than the organized discontent of the people. It was, he said, the organized aspiration of the people for a fuller, nobler, richer, kindlier life for every man, woman, and child in the ranks of humanity. The Populists, he declared, sought the enhancement of human self-fulfillment to a degree that it would not be simply temporary. "The people's party is not a passing cloud on the political sky. It is not a transient gust of popular discontent caused by bad crops or hard times. It is an uprising of principle, and the millions who have espoused these principles will not stop until they have become incorporated into the constitution of the government and the framework of society."[10] Such a view of human freedom and potential fused the concerns of Carwardine and Lloyd. Both of them stated, that the standard for judging industrial America in the 1890's ought to be the degree to which it promoted the "divinity of humanity" or produced dehumanized and impoverished men. They did not want to limit the fight, as some historians have presented it, to any one narrow issue. Instead, persons such as Lloyd and Hamlin Garland said to James B. Weaver, in the midst of his 1892 presidential campaign, "don't confine the fight to any one thing, money or land. Let's make the fight for human liberty and for the rights of men."[11] Clarence Darrow, another well known Populist-oriented personality, who spoke to the same Chicago rally as Lloyd (and who received his attitudes toward the Pullman strike mainly from Carwardine, according to some Pullman contemporaries still living) called for a more democratic industrial system. Since the workers created America's "wonderful industrial system," they certainly had a right to enjoy it, he said.

George N. Gibson, another active Populist, and editor of the *Alliance - Independent*, also corresponded with Lloyd. They both condemned the Social Darwinism of the times which created miserable conditions for the workers. Gibson wrote to Lloyd, that America must put together its property, labor, economic wisdom, knowledge and varying talents toward Christianizing and democratizing society.

Now to consider the correpsondence between Lloyd and Carwardine. On July 6, 1894, Carwardine sent a letter to Lloyd, along with a copy of a book he had just written entitled *The Pullman Strike*. This book will be analyzed in detail in a later chapter, as it is a very significant source for Carwardine's values and activities during the strike. The letter accompanying the book sent to Lloyd is significant in that it indicates the common concern of the two men. Carwardine wrote that he hoped the book would have a large circulation, for he had carefully written it "in the hope of reaching the class of people who are so prejudiced against the strikers. My book is simply an appeal of justice."[12]

In another letter addressed August 3, 1894, Carwardine noted that he had received a check for $10 from Lloyd, and that he was quite sick from overwork and stress involved in his struggle in the Pullman strike. Again he expressed a similarity of thought with Lloyd and other Populists when he wrote that there were many things he did not approve of in the labor crises, such as incidents of violence and lawlessness, but he knew that "we will have to treat the laboring classes differently in the future, or there will be more trouble."[13]

Another letter written on December 28, 1894, is of particular interest, as it shows a working relationship between Carwardine, Lloyd, and Eugene V. Debs, president of the American Railway Union which had worked for the Pullman workers during the strike. Debs was being prosecuted along with others of his union leaders for ignoring a federal injunction issued during the strike. Carwardine wrote to Lloyd:

> I received a letter yesterday from Mr. Eugene V. Debs asking if I would be willing to allow my name to be used on a committee for solicitation of funds to carry the case of the officers of the American Railway Union to the Supreme Court; and if so to notify you. I have consented to do so and here with send you my name for said committee. Without any reference to my position on the Labor Question, I am anxious to see the case carried to the Supreme Court if no other reason than one of curiosity as to the ruling of that court in the matter.[14]

Carwardine also thanked Lloyd for sending him a copy of his book, *Wealth Against Commonwealth.* He expressed agreement with Lloyd's thought, calling the book a splendid piece of work. Of particular interest was Carwardine's reaction to reviews of the book by critics who, he felt, out of closed minded prejudice, indiscriminately condemned all dissent. Carwardine wrote:

> I read 'The Nation's' criticism of your book, and was disgusted with the almost scurrilous manner in which they treated it. Such criticism is abusive - nothing discriminating or sensible about it. It is astonishing how much prejudice there is against any advanced position on the social and industrial questions of the day. I have met with my share of it, and yet it is nothing more than can be expected under the existing condition of things generally.[15]

Lloyd's response to Carwardine's letter of December 28 is interesting in that it again illustrates the empathy of the men for each other's thought. Lloyd wrote:

> I am glad that you are willing to serve on the Debs' Civil Rights Committee. I have some hopes that we shall be able to do something to stir public opinion. We need only be anxious about ourselves and our rights and not about Debs and his rights to have a sufficient inspiring motive to push this case to its conclusion. I thought 'The Nation's' review of my book was itself 'a notable instance of the rhetorical blunder of overstatement'. They say, for instance, that a dog would not be hanged on such evidence. Of course they knew that this dog had been hanged on this evidence by every court and tribunal before which he had been haled. [speaking of the Standard Oil Company] My book is almost nothing than a transcript of the adjudications proving the guilt of these men. The fact is, speaking with a purely ethical and intellectual feeling, with no possible heat, the economic functions of the successful men of the Trust is merely that of thieves; their

economic work is simply to transfer to their own possession the wealth which belongs to others and to do this without compensation, without consent, and usually in down-right violation of the statue law, and I begin to think it is about time to come out squarely and directly before the public and put this brand upon these people.[16]

Carwardine's letter to Lloyd on the 29th of August, 1895, is interesting from two points of view. As the detailed treatment of the strike later will show, George Pullman insisted that the management of his company did not require the workers to live in his town and therefore to pay rents back to it out of their pay checks. Carwardine had said that the company did demand such residence by implication if not by written law. This letter indicates that if Pullman did permit residence outside of his company town, it was not understood nor practiced until the pressure of Carwardine and others forced the issue. The letter also indicates the strong opposition to Carwardine by the company. This becomes clear as he appealed to Lloyd for financial aid for the local Pullman Methodist Church and gave his rationale for such a request. He stated that past years had been tough financially for the church, but the current year was especially so.

> Last year was bad enough but this has been worse, owing to the fact that so many people have taken advantage of the Company's position assumed last year, to the effect that they never compelled their employees to live in Pullman. We all knew that to be false; hence this year a great number have moved out, living elsewhere. Consequently my church year is closing with a debt of $400,000 on our hands. I am making every effort to meet this by an appeal to my friends. With our heavy rent of $500.00 it has been a severe struggle for us. The Company has a very bitter feeling toward me, on account

of my position toward them, and it has been a source of annoyance to them to see me hold my own here during the past conference year, sustained as I have been by the denomination at large.[17]

Lloyd and his wife responded to Carwardine's request and in so doing gave evidence of how Carwardine's social gospel (applied Christianity) was related to his labor and Populism orientation as manifested in the Pullman strike. They wrote: 'Mrs Lloyd and I are glad to be able to contribute our mite to so good a cause as the upholding of 'applied Christianity' in deed as well as word at Pullman. Have you published anything about the situation there additional to your first book?"[18]

Carwardine, upon receiving the Lloyds' letter and contribution, replied on September 10, 1895, thanking them, and saying he wished there were some way he could express his gratitude. He decided that the most meaningful expression of thanks would be to continue his common cause with Lloyd. Again their common basis of concern was expressed as Carwardine wrote:

I wish it was in my power to do something for you by way of thanks. The best I can do is to keep on working along the lines of 'applied Christianity'. It is wonderful what a change is coming over many of our preachers. Just a year ago they were, some of them, ready to oust me from the Conference as an 'anarchist'. Today they are telling me I am just right and many of them (though not all) are discussing these industrial questions as never before. I have written nothing further on the Pullman question since issuing my book; but I have done considerable lecturing on the Pullman matter."[19]

Carwardine also expressed a desire to meet Lloyd for a discussion of their concerns, along with some of Carwardine's friends on the faculty of the University of Chicago.

Carwardine's letter to Lloyd on April 21, 1896, is of importance for many reasons. He answered Lloyd's request for a list of Chicago area ministers to whom he could send copies of his book, again illustrating the concern to influence leaders among the "prejudiced groups" in order to turn their influence toward the "cause." Carwardine again thanked Lloyd for his favors and common sympathy, and sought means to further influence the publics' minds. Carwardine was to become very active in writing newspaper columns, and in this letter he sought Lloyd's advice on the matter. He wrote: "Are you a member of the Chicago Press Club? If so, do you know whether I could be admitted to membership? Do the rules admit of members, outside of the direct newspaper fraternity? When you have leisure, please let me know, and if I am eligible, and decide to join, would you be willing to propose my name?" Further in the letter, Carwardine mentioned his intention of writing a novel, related to labor problems, in addition to his book, *The Pullman Strike*. As will be seen when the strike is dealt with in detail, the motive for his desire to write a novel was the common response of the Pullman Company to labor's demands, "nothing to arbitrate". Carwardine wrote:

> I have long contemplated writing a story, bearing upon matters
> connected with the labor problem. I have thought of giving it
> the title, 'Nothing to Arbitrate'. It seems to me that a good
> novel of that kind, ought to take, especially among the laboring
> classes. Do you think there would be any demand for
> something of the kind?"[20]

It is interesting that at this point, along with the desire to reach and influence public opinion, Carwardine would not mind selling a few books among the workers he represented. Certainly their concern in his cause combined with his barbed attacks should create a situation where his novel "ought to take."

Lloyd picked up the double cause in writing such a novel when he responded to Carwardine's letter. Encouraging him to join the Chicago Press Club, though he himself was not a member, he went on to say: "I feel sure that a novel from you on the labor movement would command wide reading and do a great deal of good; and I think your title is a very good one. I doubt if the laboring classes would read any very great number of the book, as I do not think they do much in the way of book buying. But the book buying public, I am sure, will welcome it."[21] There is no evidence that Carwardine ever wrote the novel, "Nothing to Arbitrate."

Finally, the letter that Carwardine wrote on May 5, 1906, to Mrs. C. L. Withington, Lloyd's sister, shows the common concern of the two men. This letter was written after Lloyd had died, and read: "Your dear brother was very kind to me in the days of the Pullman Industrial shuffle (1894), and we met many times thereafter. I admired and esteemed him highly. His death was a severe loss to all interested in the social welfare of humanity."[22]

Concerning Carwardine's Populist/Progressive orientation, it is interesting to note that prior to his Illinois pastorates, he had served pastorates in the heavily Populist-oriented state of Kansas. He had been a member of the South Kansas Annual Conference of the Methodist Episcopal Church, and had served pastorates in Kansas from 1882 to 1887. Lorenzo D. Lewelling was governor of Kansas, and was very vocal in demanding that American society must distinguish between human rights and property rights. He said of the Gilded Age, that it had so much regard for the rights of property that it had forgotten the liberties of the individual. Kansas newspapers were constantly filled with Populist articles stating that they wanted to make the United States an "industrialized democracy." They were not interested in opposing industrialism as such, but only its abuses as symbolized by the monopolies and the distortion of traditional values. They wanted an industrial democracy where every citizen had an equal interest. Again Governor Lewelling said, in a speech given in Kansas City: "It is the business of the Government to make it possible for me to live and sustain the life of my family. It is the duty of government to protect the weak, because the strong are able to protect themselves."[23]

Lewelling and others in Kansas were emphasizing that the success myth, laissez faire capitalism, and Social Darwinism had to be rejected. Unbridled individualism, they said, destroyed instead of promoted the general welfare. Therefore many Populists suggested a substitution of co-operation and mutual help for rugged competition and self-help. This, they said, led to true individualism. Instead of having the corporation absorb the community, it was necessary for the community to absorb the corporation. They condemned the paternalism of the captains' of industry trusteeship and the enslavement of the masses by the reigning plutocracy. "The horror of 'paternalism' hangs like a black pall over the buried hopes of the helpless poor."[24]

Frank Doster was an active and powerful Populist leader in Kansas, who insisted that the Republican and Democratic parties were paralyzed and hypnotized into inactivity by the power of monopolies. Therefore he called for political action outside the two main parties. He called for pressure upon the federal government to do for the individual what he could not successfully do for himself or to do for the individual what others would not do on just and equitable terms. He insisted that the industrial system of the nation should, like the political system, be of, for, and by the people alone.

It was in such an environment that Carwardine lived and worked. He nurtured his own Populist/Progressive thinking and manifested it clearly in the Pullman strike.

Before dealing with the Pullman strike in detail, a few speeches and articles from Carwardine should be considered which span the period during and after the strike. The purpose is to clearly set forth his value orientation so as to form a context within which his role in the strike may be more meaningfully understood.

Carwardine lashed out at those who would call strikers and reformers such as himself anarchists. In so doing, he illustrated his Populist/Progressive orientation. The real anarchists, he insisted, were not strikers driven to action by atrocious working conditions. The real anarchists were the monopolists and capitalists, "who, while professing to respect the law, use it as a means to steal from others." Black listing he cited as the worst kind of anarchy, which should have been considered a penal offense. Workers were forced to wander through the country as a result of black listing, "as if he were an escaped convict, with a price upon his head. I can tell you of men who went from place to place in vain."[25]

In a potent speech given on February 23, 1897, Carwardine condemned monopolies and government by millionaires. Speaking in Memorial Hall, Toledo, Ohio, at a labor gathering sponsored by the Central Labor Union, and being presented to the crowd by E. P. Usher, president of the Union, he referred to the terrible suffering where in the shadow of plenty, thousands starved. Monopolies, he said, had obtained such a position of power that the poor had little chance. He reminded the crowd that America's labor force was the foundation of the country. He stated that the labor situation was at a crisis stage, but he felt it could be solved without bloodshed. The country was a "seething, foaming caldron of dissatisfaction. Men call each other anarchists, and some go so far as to predict that we are on the verge of a revolution." Citing a few statistics, he pointed out that one-half of the wealth in the United States was owned by 25,000 persons, or one-seventieth of the population, many of whom were related to trusts. "It would not surprise me to hear next of the millionaires buying up all the shafts in heaven and running a heaven trust."[26]

Carwardine cited the admission a few years earlier by a Mr. Haveyezer, that thousands of dollars had been spent in getting elected to Congress men favorable to the trusts' interests. Government, he said, was more or less controlled by multi-millionaires. In McKinley's cabinet for example, every member except two were millionaires. Meanwhile, in the sweat shops of New York and Chicago, unfortunate laborers made $1 to $2 a week while skilled laborers would have been in nearly as bad a position were it not for trade unions. He declared the cardinal principles of the trade unions to have been right, "and the workingman who will not support his union is less than a man."[27] Venal politicians, he said, manipulated votes and legislation, so that wealth was legislated out of the pockets of the masses into the coffers of the wealthy. This must be stopped.

While wealth increased, wages decreased. The end result was that "we have three classes, the laboring class, the middle class and the enormously wealthy. The danger is not between the first and the second, but between the first and the third."

Carwardine was very determined to impress upon people that what he was doing and saying was not anarchistic, un-American, or subversive but indeed was being done because he wanted America to be the great Republic it was meant to be and could be. For example, when he spoke to the graduating summer school class in LaSalle, Illinois, where he was pastor in June, 1896, he spoke of the value of education for the well-being of society. The address was definitely Populist-flavored. He laid forth what he felt would lead to a successful government and especially an effective Republic.

A Republic, he said, was where the people made the laws that governed them, and "depends absolutely upon the intelligence of its citizens. The state must educate as a matter of self-protection." Ignorance could be endured under an absolute monarchy as in Russia, but never under a republican form of government. Ignorant citizens were a menace to the success of any government, "but under a constitution such as ours, ignorance is a monstrous evil." He then addressed the students pointedly and said: "Now I want you ever to be proud of this system of popular education, which is indeed the bulwark of our liberties." He encouraged the students to set their goals high, as Emerson meant by the words, "hitch your wagon to a star." No one, he said, could measure the possibilities of youthful ambition.[28]

In many of his speeches and newspaper articles, Carwardine lashed out at the corporations and the distorted values they propagated. He felt the corporation removed the moral element from businessmen, who would do things on a board of directors that they would not do as individual person. For example, as individual persons, they would worship and live good lives, but as corporate directors, they would rob, lie, and bribe. As individual persons they would act with patriotic love for their country, while as corporate directors they would debauch state legislatures and put false evaluation assessments on property. As individuals, they would give millions of dollars to the poor, while as corporation directors they would reduce wages to the point of starvation. "The corporation is the most perfect form of absolute monarchy - and a monarchy without a soul." He did not however advocate the abolition of all corporations or capitalism as such.

Corporations with limitations to their power and methods may
be a necessary factor in modern civilization, but when a
corporation tramples upon the rights and privileges of citizens,
keeps up its dividends by cutting the wages of its employees

to starving point, violates the law of the state in various ways, and corrupts the political conscience of a people, then it becomes dangerous to society and ought to be rebuked.[29]

Carwardine picked up another Populist-oriented theme when he emphasized a need for the inheritance tax to be properly regulated and related it to his attack on the corporation. "Corporate power is a menace to the welfare of a community when it seeks to evade the just assessment valuation of its property." He went on to give some examples of extreme violations of the law in this direction in Chicago.

Our newspapers have given extended publicity to this end, and a great outcry has been made on this subject. Not only ought the corporation to be made to bear its full share of the burden of the state, but I believe in a system of taxation by which the burdens of government shall fall upon all the people alike, and thus cause the wealthier classes to bear the greater share of that burden in accordance with the principles of equity and justice. We ought to have a properly regulated inheritance tax, and I believe, in spite of the supreme court decisions on the subject that an income tax justly levied and enforced would be a very proper law in this country (the Pullman case - $200,000 tax less than what it should be). The rights of property are now warring on the rights of man."[30]

Carwardine's Populist beliefs became vivid when he discussed the stages of the workers' development. Three steps, he said, had marked the upward trend of the workingman toward industrial freedom: from slavery, to vassalage, to employment. The next step would be that embodied in the idea of the co-operative commonwealth, joint proprietorship, profit-sharing, and basing the conditions of society on the ethical principles of the "Sermon on the Mount." "The day is coming when the world will look back on the competitive wages system with the same abhorrence with which we now look back upon the feudal system and slavery."[31]

Certainly fitting for his Populist mind was his emphasis on the need for the government to take a vital role in regulation, and in spite of the abuse he felt he received for his position, he felt he and others of his mind must continue the attacks. "They are slaves who fear to speak, for the fallen or the weak," he would often say. He warned that it would be suicide for the government to ignore the labor problem and not take a more active role in regulation. "The nation that disregards its labor element is like the man who draws the keen razor across his own throat." Labor, he insisted, was the foundation of the nation, and in the midst of labor unrest, the government must take up responsibility for curing its ills. "The ship of state never needed truer pilots than now. The United States of 1895-6-7 is a far different country from the United States of 1864, or the colonies of 1776."[32] The government must regulate on behalf of a man's right to a day's work at a fair day's wage. The situation was approaching a crisis stage, warned Carwardine, and the government could no longer pretend that unlike the "old countries," the United States had no problems. Thus he was attacking the evolved and distorted American values of nature, providence, and will which had led to a laissez faire naturalism which asserted all was well, and all would always be well, because the United States had broken from the European perspective and "Old World" decadence. Carwardine warned that this popularly held polarity between American progressiveness and European barbarism was false optimism. "We see on all sides of us evidences of the worst depths of barbarism."

Of course in the midst of his active speech making and writing, Carwardine was often, as cited earlier, accused of being an anarchist. He was able to take the accusations in stride, for he felt anyone who considered himself to be right and sided with a minority position would be accused of such. After he and some of his friends had been accused of anarchism, he humorously said that "he himself had had the most delectable experience of being called an anarchist though he knew of nothing anarchistic about himself except his red hair."

Carwardine went on, from his criticism of the status quo and call for government regulation, to advocate many specific programs similar to those of the Populists discussed earlier. He advocated the eight hour work day, government ownership of railroads and similar enterprises, co-operative plans of living, state boards of arbitration, abolition of government by injunction, and above all, active political participation. Concerning government by injunction, he cited Eugene Debs as the "heroic martyr to government by injunction." As to the right to vote, he said: "Use it as the Godgiven gift to you, as a token of your rights as men. Do not let professional politicians use you as a man does an orange which, when sucked of its juice, he throws away. Let your vote be all that is highest in freedom, in citizenship. It is the only solution."[33]

There appears to be yet another significant influence upon the value orientation of Carwardine - Christian socialism.

-CHRISTIAN SOCIALISM-

Socialism, within our context, refers to the general political and economic theories that advocate a system of collective or government ownership and management of the means of production and distribution of goods, and is contrasted to the doctrine of the sanctity of property in private (and corporate) hands that is characteristic of capitalism.

There have been numerous varieties of socialism, and Christian socialism is one of these, with many varieties itself. The early English Christian socialists, Frederick Denison Maurice and Charles Kingsley, who advocated the establishment of cooperative workshops based on Christian principles, indirectly influenced Carwardine. Christian socialism in England and the United States, grew out of the conflicts between Christian ideals and the manifestations and effects of competitive capitalistic business. We are primarily concerned with English and U.S. manifestations of Christian socialism, and not European Christian socialism which most commonly refers to party or trade unions directed by *religious* leaders in contrast to socialist unions and parties.

Influential among English Christian socialists was Charles Kingsley, 1819-1875, an English author and clergyman, who in 1859 was made chaplain to Queen Victoria, from 1860 to 1869 was professor of modern history at Cambridge, and in 1873 was appointed canon of Westminster. He began publishing tracts advocating Christian socialism from 1848 to 1852, and embodied these views in two novels, *Alton Locke* (1850) and *Yeast* (1851). He applied Christian socialism to contemporary social problems in England. In later novels, such as *Hypatia* (1853), *Westward Ho!* (1855), and *Hereward the Wake* (1866), he used historical settings to communicate his Christian socialism.[34]

Another influential Christian socialist in England was Frederick Denison Maurice (1805-72), also a clergyman and social reformer, who held professorships at Kings College in London and Cambridge.

An influence upon Kingsley and Maurice, and of import to social scientists concerned about social justice, was Claude Henri de Rouvroy Saint-Simon (1760-1825), the French social philosopher, who as a young man had served in the American Revolution as a volunteer with the colonists. He was concerned about the social injustices accompanying industrialization, and called for the reorganization of society by scientists and industrialists on the basis of the "new Christianity." This new Christianity would entail a scientific division of labor resulting in automatic and spontaneous social harmony, so he idealistically thought. In 1825, he wrote a book, *The New*

Christianity, in which he asserted that any hope for the development of true brotherhood must accompany scientific organization.

It is significant to know that August Comte, the "father of sociology," whose credo "To know in order to predict and to predict in order to control," whose interest in developing a science of humankind to help in moving toward the creation of "the good society," was for a time a pupil of Saint-Simon in his salon for scientists. Saint-Simon's influence on Comte is obvious. Saint-Simon foreshadowed the positivism of Comte, and contributed ideas on socialism, a federation of the nations of Europe for mutual betterment, etc. A small group of his followers, later known as Saint-Simonians, modified and elucidated his principles into a system of thought referred to as Saint-Simonianism. They promoted the abolition of individual inheritance rights, public control of means of production, and gradual emancipation of women.[35] They influenced later socialist thought, including that of Carwardine.

Christian socialism saw a revival in England at the end of the 19th century, and it appears that the primary motivations were two-fold and interdependent. On the one hand were the problems of a rapidly industrializing society, with the accompanying problems of the "Gilded Age," social injustices, inequitable distribution of resources and goods, class stratification, etc. and the accompanying materialistic, consumptive, secularized popular culture; and on the other hand the alienation of the masses from organized religion which seemed to lose its relevancy, did not address the needs of the masses effectively, appeared often to provide a "sacred canopy" over the Gilded Age capitalism, and did not have the sensate appeal of the new popular value structure. Therefore, Christian socialists at the end of the 19th century were addressing the needs of an industrialized society and a faltering church. An additional pressure was the growing appeal of the Social Gospel, fed by those phenomena just mentioned as well as various discoveries of science, Biblical criticism, and comparative religion studies.[36]

It is also interesting to consider just why the term "Christian socialism" was chosen by these religious activists in the latter 1800's. A couple contributing factors appear clear. On the one hand, there was a revival of socialist interest proper at the end of the 19th century in England, so to incorporate the name socialism was a bit fashionable and less stigmatic than at other times. Also, in the face of declining numbers of people attending church, it seems that some ministers felt the term "socialist" would help attract workingmen back to the churches, since revived socialism was attractive to them as propagated from other sources. (A good case of impression management?)

Many Christian socialist organizations appeared in late 19th century England, among them being the Anglo-Catholic Guild of St. Matthew in 1877 (advocating "sacramental socialism" which affirmed that the best witness of Christ's socialism was in the Holy Sacraments); the Church Socialist League, 1906; The Christian Social Union, 1889; the Community of the Resurrection, 1892; the Christian Socialist Society, 1886; the Christian Socialist League, 1894; the Christian Social Brotherhood, 1898; the Free Church Socialist League, 1909; New-Church Socialist Society, 1896; Socialist Quaker Society, 1898; the Christian Socialist Fellowship, 1909; the Labour Church; the Catholic Social Guild; Catholic Socialist Societies; etc.

The many Christian socialist organizations in England manifested the situation Carwardine also addressed in Chicago, and that was that not only was there a social, economic, political crisis and various injustices accompanying industrialization, but there was a crisis in the leadership of many churches. Many religious leaders had so accommodated to the popular culture, that "they cared less about the material and spiritual welfare of the working class than the workers were alleged to care about religion. Alienation was a two-way relationship."[37]

Christian socialism, then, at the end of the 19th century, was a part of the general socialist and reform revival underway. However, it was certainly possible that Christians, like others, could become socialists for a variety of reasons. There were Christians who just happened to be socialists, and there were socialists who just happened to be Christians. However, there were also those who were peculiarly "Christian socialists," who were socialists *because* they were Christians. These people tried to develop uniquely Christian grounds for their socialist convictions, and Peter Jones, in his book *The Christian Socialist Revival*, feels that in reviewing spokesmen from the various organizations mentioned above, Christian socialists active during the end of the 19th century, usually stood for one or more of these theological arguments, or variations of them:

1. From patristics: that many of the church fathers were socialists and communists.

2. From the New Testament and the ethics of the Sermon on the Mount: that Jesus Christ was a socialist.

3. From the sacraments and the Book of Common Prayer: that the modern church in its worship, symbol, and ritual exhibits a socialist faith.

4. From the doctrine of Divine Immanence: that God's presence everywhere, in nature and in man, destroys the artificial distinction between the "sacred" and the "secular" worlds, sanctifies the material life, and supports the socialist call for a Kingdom of God on earth.[38]

It is at this point that a major problem running through Christian socialism should be cited, and that is the common problem of integrating a general, theoretical and/or theological critique or analysis of societal conditions into realistic, implementable programs and policies. Unfortunately, then as now, it is easier to critique and theorize than to implement a program that is pragmatically useful.

For example, consider Stewart Headlam, founder of the Guild of St. Matthew, at its peak strength in 1894-95. He said of Jesus Christ:

...when you worship Him you are worshipping the Savior, the social and political Emancipator, the greatest of all secular workers, the founder of the great socialistic society for the promotion of righteousness, the preacher of a revolution, the denouncer of kings, the gentle, tender sympathizer with the rough and the outcast, who could utter scathing, burning words against the rich, the respectable, the religious.[39]

At the Guild's eleventh annual meeting, September of 1888, Headlam cited five principles that he felt Christ taught by his own actions:

1. the importance of work in this world

2. the need sometimes to be aggressive, even "stern" and "violent" in language

3. that Christ is King of all spheres of human activity

4. that the Church was intended to be "an organized Brotherhood" for the extension of social justice

5. that "the eternal Word of God speaks to many who do not know that it is His voice.[40]

The problem for Headlam was, and the social scientist is, the "how" of implementing such principles into programs and policies, lest the principles appear rather esoteric, aloof, naive, and idealistic, and lest they remain "theoretical" but "non-implementable." This same problem appears in the thought and activities of Carwardine and contemporary Christian socialists.

Christian Socialists in the United States

Christian socialists in the United States toward the end of the 1800's, much as those in Britain, were critical that religion had been so preoccupied with theology that it had become indifferent to questions concerning social justice. Dogma seemed to take precedence over ethics. It is interesting to note that many early U. S. Christian socialists came from Calvinist churches, whose theology did have a "this-worldly" thrust, where the "Kingdom of God" carried ethical implications for the transformation of "this world" into a more righteous and just society. It was asserted that too often the church became so preoccupied with the saving of individuals, that it ignored the "saving of society," and that unless a "corrupted society" were corrected it would continue to corrupt individuals. Certainly there are similarities in those critics and those sociologists who emphasize the impact of environment and learning on individual behavior.

However, most of these early Christian socialists suffered a trait that seems to run through Christian socialists from beginning to end. They understood and encouraged "gradualism" and "reformation" as opposed to "revolution" to the point that their call for change often amounted to little less than a plea for some vague "organic unity of the race" or piecemeal reform.[41] They seemed to feel that socialism would "evolve" naturally as a stage in ongoing social evolution, with the help of logical moral persuasion and humanity's natural capacity to respond to the "good."

They seemed to be afraid of the possible consequences of their call for justice, afraid of "revolution" instead of "evolution," and naively adhered to humanity's natural response to moral persuasion. They underestimated the resistance of selfish vested interest groups. Therefore, most of them promoted the general upholding of law and order, and opposed rebellion or revolt. As Dombrowski states in his book, *The Early Days of Christian Socialism in America*:

> When the good-will ethic was translated into a practical strategy it took the form of upholding law and order and opposing all forms of rebellion and revolt. The net result was that social Christianity was delivered into the hands of the ruling class as one more instrument for keeping the proletarian group quiescent.[42]

Might this be a classic case of co-optation? These early Christian socialists suffered from a disease similar to that of many contemporary optimistic, idealistic and naive "reformers" and that is the underestimation of the power and resistance of entrenched vested interest groups, especially in the corporate realm, whose advantage it is to leave things as they are. Entrenched vested interest groups do not readily respond to moral, humanitarian persuasion if it implies a change in their positions of advantage. There were, of course, the "exceptional" Christian socialists such as the Rev. George D. Herron, onetime professor of applied Christianity, Grinnell College, in Grinnell, Iowa, who wrote "The Social System and the Christian Conscience" in *The Kingdom*, August 18, 1898. Herron believed that economic interests often dominated other realms, including the moral, and caused the moral and religious realms to develop rationales for the economic interests of business vested interest groups. Economics conditioned ethical attitudes, said Herron, so how can we obey Christ's law of love when every industrial maxim, custom, fact and principle renders that law inoperative.[43]

Herron believed that the primary task of religion was to revolutionize the economic base of society, but not too many Christian sociologists wanted to push the implication of this thought to its seemingly logical conclusion!

Herron did push it to its logical conclusion, as he saw it. He saw Christianity and socialism as mutual allies, and the duty of Christians was the destruction of capitalism. (He was, of course, forced from his professorship and from the Congregational ministry.)

> Both Christianity and socialism fight for a socialized world in order that a co-operative society may replace a competitive profit-seeking order, freeing men to labor for the common welfare; that material goods may be devoted to the material and cultural development of all the workers rather than to the creation of profits for the few; that a classless world may be established, with no divisive social lines to destroy the spirit of brotherhood which can only operate in a profound manner in a society which approaches an egalitarian principle; in a word, that the good life may be made available universally and human beings, wherever found, may be assured of opportunity for the fullest development of all latent potentialities. Socialism is based on the actual operation of the law of love and may take the place of religion for those who look upon religion as brotherhood, mutual support in seeking the good life.[44]

Herron realized the naivety in those who thought that through moral persuasion those "at the top" would willingly redistribute resources and goods. He saw the reality of class struggle and that change would come only when workers organized and created enough "conflict" to "force" change. Herron would fit nicely into the contemporary "conflictionist" perspective.

Herron was one of the few Christian socialists, unlike Carwardine who took issue with Herron at this point, who would not rule out violent revolution as "a Christian solution." Peace at the expense of justice, he felt, was not a religious solution to social problems. He could tolerate a revolution by violence, if it promised a more just society. "It will not do to say that revolution is not coming, or pronounce it of the devil. Resolutions even in their wildest forms, are the impulses of God moving in tides of fire through the life of man."[45]

Richard T. Ely, who was a contemporary of Herron, and was a professor of economics at Johns Hopkins University and the University of Wisconsin, was a major influence on Carwardine. His books, *Social Aspects of Christianity* and *Introduction to Political Economy*, were required reading for men entering the Methodist ministry, which Carwardine did. Ely was a main supporter of the American Economics Association, which viewed laissez-faire economics as dangerous and immoral and a perpetuator of class conflict. Ely encouraged the application of sociological studies to industrial problems, and felt theological seminaries should become intellectual centers for the study of sociology. Ely, however, unlike Herron but more like most other Christian socialists, including Carwardine, was greatly influenced by a belief in "natural progress" in evolutionary development, which led him to denounce revolution and promote reform guided by charity and benevolence. Ely hoped for "Christianity coupled with Nationalism," a free and peaceful evolution of industrial institutions, and not a radical departure from fundamental institutions. He believed, unlike Herron, that there was not a rigid class struggle in the United States, that moral persuasion could do the job, and that controlling vested interest groups would, through moral persuasion, relinquish power voluntarily. Again, there seems to be a naive and unrealistic lack of appreciation for the rigidity of vested interest groups.

Dombrowski, who, like most other researchers studying this period of time (and like others were unaware of Carwardine's activities and importance) recognized this problem among Christian socialists in general. In his book, *The Early Days of Christian Socialism in America*, Dombrowski writes, concerning Ely's advice for peace, contentment, and respect for law and order because the "right is bound to win:"

> All of the fallacies of liberalism that have made radical religion and the labor movement in this country so impotent for the past fifty years are exhibited in this 'final word of advice,' which unfortunately was taken to heart by the representatives of labor and social Christianity.[46]

Let us look at another early Christian socialist who influenced Carwardine and who also promoted the application of a value-laden sociology to problems of social injustice. W. D. P. Bliss, a Congregational minister as was Herron, was the key figure in the Society of Christian Socialists. At an organizational meeting in 1889, a Declaration of Principles was drawn, which characterized capitalism as a dangerous plutocracy based on economic individualism, and promoted instead a new order based on a more equitable distribution of resources. The Society of Christian Socialists endeavored to show that the aim of socialism was embraced in the aim of Christianity and tried to convince Christians that the teachings of Jesus led directly to a form of socialism.

Christians must, the Society advocated, demand a reconstructed social order, "which, adopting *some method* of production and distribution that starts from organized society as a body and seeks to benefit society equitably in every one of its members, shall be based on the Christian principle that 'We are members one of another'"[47] (italics are mine). Again you see the problem of defining just what the implications of such statements are in terms of specific, implementable programs and policies!

For a short period of time, Bliss promoted "colonies" or "union farms" as a way to reform society. However, one theme was consistently present in Bliss, and that was the need to wed sociology and theology! Christianity somehow implied a united co-operative society, and sociology was to assist in analyzing the present problems and the "how" of change.

Bliss, although lacking specific programs and policies, did make three recommendations for action on the part of Christian socialists:

1.   Personal living: the Christian socialist was to live life simply, giving up time, money, and position if necessary for his convictions (many did this, such as Herron, Carwardine, etc.)

2.   Social work: he was to educate, agitate, and organize; to distribute literature and speak whenever the opportunity arose; to promote labor organizations and to *join a radical political party*.

3.   Work for reform legislation: by promoting such measures as the Australian ballot, single-tax measures, free technical education, free meals for school children, public ownership of utilities, and so forth...these measures were only first steps toward the *ultimate economic revolution* toward which they must work.[48] (italics are mine)

For the purpose of pointing out that Bliss did encourage program and policy in as much as he encouraged joining a "radical political party," but often these parties themselves lacked specific programs. Frequently, though Christian socialists spoke of the "ultimate economic revolution" (obviously value-laden), they ended up only dabbling in petty reform proposals, and the "ultimate revolution" was greatly obscured. Bliss, as others, was too much an idealist, evolutionist, and gradualist to see the real "radicalness" implied in his theory, and was unnerved by the potential "anarchy and confusion" of "extreme socialism." Change must not come too fast!

However, the end goal of "gradual socialism" held radical implications compared to the present economic ordering of things. Bliss, for example, saw the goal to be the national, state, or local owning of land and capital collectively and operating it co-operatively for the equitable good of all.

There did develop a "radical religious press" to carry the thoughts of Christian socialism and other "radical ideologists," notably *The Dawn* and *The Kingdom*. Much of the above thoughts, that of Bliss and others, was carried in these papers.

Finally, a word should be said about Henry Demarest Lloyd. He and Carwardine corresponded and mutually influenced each other. Lloyd gave moral and financial assistance to Carwardine in the midst of his Pullman Strike activities. Lloyd was an influential newspaper editor in Chicago, and spent much time analyzing the unethical ideology and practice of the business community in the latter 1800's, and also the responsibility of religious leaders in the social justice arena. For example, he directed his criticism toward the Standard Oil Company through the *Atlantic Monthly*, and expanded this into a book, *Wealth Against Commonwealth*, published in 1894, the year of the Pullman Strike. He supported various colony plans, but had the vision to see that they were not the total answer, that socialism and its goals could not be fulfilled via piecemeal reform. Embodying a good sociological principle, the recognition that we live our lives in groups and institutions, Lloyd emphasized that attention had to be placed on changing *institutions*, not simply individuals. He saw that economic concerns seemed to be the dominant ones, and that real change required changing economic institutions before morals, required destroying the present economic philosophy and system dominated by corporate vested interests.

Lloyd, while appreciating those promoting "brotherly love" as a tool in the struggle, also recognized the resistance to change by vested interest groups. They could not be moved by moral appeal alone -coercion was necessary. (Lloyd would have made a good conflictionist!) He felt the value of peace and nonresistance must not be given precedence over social justice. "There is but one evil greater than reform by force - the perpetuation, the permanence of injustice."[49] As he became older, Lloyd became more and more disillusioned with gradualism and piecemeal reform. He voted Socialist in 1896 and 1900, and was about to openly publicly align himself with the Socialist Party in 1903, when he died.

His notebook entries for 1903 manifested his frustration and new commitment, especially when he wrote:

> Christianity is the religion that was, socialism is the religion
> that is to be... Our old politics, Democratic and Republican,
> rest on habit, the persistence of organization, on the bribes of
> money, on power, on selfish self-interest, but there is no
> heartbeat in them, no hope or love.[50]

For those persons actively interested in moving toward the creation of more social justice, and looking for tools to do so, this suggestion of Lloyd's merits careful consideration, specifically the need for another political party. This party would need enough numbers and clout to make itself, and force the other two parties, capable of addressing social injustice and forming programs and policies to rectify them and to break the strangle hold of corporate vested interest ideology and structure which prohibits a more equitable distribution of resources and goods.

The Christian Social Union, with branches in Chicago, Minnesota, Philadelphia, Iowa, Boston, New York City, and Omaha promoted a "Christianized State." Again, of course, there arises the problem of defining and implementing a "Christianized State." There is another very contemporary issue here which is part of the separation of the church and state question, and that is the "correctness" and "legality" of implementing a program or policy that is a direct manifestation of a particular religious faith commitment, when the nation itself consists of such religious and non-religious heterogeneity.

There were assumptions that Carwardine and many Christian Socialists in the U.S. held in common, such as the necessity for trade unions, the belief that isolated labor meant enslaved labor, old age pensions, co-operative production, the belief that power lay in organization, and that combination helped to moralize workers and better their condition.

However, there was lacking a genuine, integrated, holistic kind of Christian socialist economic policy, and a program that would help achieve access to the power needed to implement the goals envisioned. These are the kinds of problems that one finds time and again in the study of reform and civil rights movements.

The Church Socialist League was another influential organization for those who sought to apply their faith toward the establishment of social justice. The Church Socialist League consisted of church people who accepted the principles of socialism in terms of advocating the political, economic and social emancipation of the whole people by establishing a "democratic commonwealth in which the community shall own the land and capital collectively" and use them for the good of all people."[51]

The principles of the Church Socialist League were:

1. The Church had a mission to the whole of human life, social and individual, material and spiritual.

2. The Church can best fulfill its social mission by acting in its corporate capacity.

3. To this end the members of the League accept the principle of socialism.

4. Socialism is the fixed principle according to which the community should own the land and capital collectively, and use them co-operatively for the good of all.[52]

These principles were also widely held by Christian socialists, including Carwardine, and manifested the same problem of moving from the realm of idealism and a naivety to offering a comprehensive, holistic program of "how!"

There was a degree of divisiveness in the Church Socialist League that is of great contemporary import, and relates to one of the assertions made at the outset concerning the degree of involvement by sociologists in implementing the implications of social research into value-laden programs designed to help bring about social justice. One member of the Church Socialist League, the Rev. P. E. T. Widdrington, wished to develop a "Christian sociology," that is a Christian study of society. He was chastised by other members as being too prone to "intellectualism," too prone to "armchair socialism," and too little prone to be active in a pragmatic program on the behalf of or to identify personally with, the larger labor movement.

The aims of the Christian Socialist Society, at its founding in 1886, echo similar concerns as other organizations discussed so far:

1. The union of men in a real universal brotherhood free from all artificial distinctions founded merely upon class.

2. Education, liberal, free, compulsory, industrial, for all.

3. Substitution of a system of production for use for the present system of production for profit.

4. The organization of society on a basis of industry and manual worth, rather than of wealth, privilege and monopoly as at present; industry being understood to comprise both mental and manual work.

5. Public control of land, capital and all means of production, distribution and exchange, involving the abolition of all interest.

6. The ennobling of domestic, public and national life; the development of free and independent nationalities; the union of labor; and the promotion of peace and goodwill all over the world.[53]

Again, the really difficult task would be the "how" of implementing such a program within the context of a system dominated by very strong vested interest groups. E. D. Girdlestone suggested his approach as to the "how" of implementing such a program, easier said than done, and that was through "effective socialization." This raises such questions as to the possibility of "re-socialization" in the midst of such diverse and previous conditioning, and just how far and by what means one should go to implement such re-socialization. In his book, *The What and Why of Christian Socialism*, Girdlestone called for the socialization of both men and institutions. He felt a truly Christian socialism should aim to socialize the individual from the nursery upwards by socializing the educational system.[54]

This proposal raises another contemporary issue, the possibility of such "re-socialization," and the morality of methods used. For example, does the end justify any means for bringing about such a re-socialization, even if the end were considered good and necessary?

Bruce Wallace proposed an interesting program, called the Brotherhood Trust. The Brotherhood Trust was a complex cooperative structure which was to carry on trade and industry, and from its profits pay good trade-union wage rates to all its workers, along with old-age pensions, sickness and accident benefits, etc. The goal was to build a complete cooperative colony with its own farms, factories, stores, and homes. It was planned that the Trust would organize a million members into one great "cooperative commonwealth" and *shame the capitalist system into surrender.*[55]

Although the hope of "shaming the capitalist system into surrender" was extremely naive and did not appreciate the rigidity of vested interest self-preservation, there have been and are cooperative ventures which draw upon Wallace's concepts.

It is interesting to note that English Methodism, like U.S. Methodism, did not produce many Christian socialists considering the size of the denomination. One of the vocal English Methodist Christian socialists, who perhaps influenced Carwardine, was the Rev. Hugh Price Hughes, who established the "*Methodist Times*" in 1885 as a "journal of religious and social movement." Hughes wanted to promote egalitarianism, and wanted to remove the middle-class, employer-class "taint" from Methodism.

His Christian socialism was simple and Christ-centered, and sounded very much like that of Carwardine (or perhaps Carwardine sounded very much like Hughes). For example:

'Jesus Christ was essentially a man of the People - a working
man...the laws and policies of States must be subjected to the
teaching of Jesus Christ.' Christ's love extended to everyone,
whatever his class or condition: 'a harlot is dying in a back
slum....That harlot is as dear to Christ as the Queen of

England herself....Let us once realize the sacredness of every human being, however poor, however ignorant, however degraded, and tyranny becomes impossible, lust becomes impossible, war becomes impossible. This is the new idea which Jesus Christ introduced into human society.' [56]

Those persons concerned for social justice would drool over envisioning such a state of affairs as Hughes described, but alas is left despairing that the picture is extremely wishful and naive, and only possible if all persons everywhere operated from the same cluster of values and of commitment. Since this seems not a likely possibility, we are left with the same question: how can Christian socialism be implemented into a concrete, pragmentic policy and program.

Carwardine's alienation from oppressive vested interest groups developed early in his childhood, as he described in his book, *The Pullman Strike*:

I well remember, when as orphan boy in the city of New York, having to work for six years under an abusive foreman in the composing room of the New York Evening Post. Of all the men I have ever met, he was the embodiment of tyranny, a man of considerable ability, but foul in language and despotic authority, the daily terror of all who were under his influence. He treated men like dogs, swore at them and abused them without stint. In those days there was engendered in my soul a hatred against tyrannical foremen and abusive treatment of men which has never left me, and which during the past months of our long and sad winter, (during the Pullman Strike of 1894) made my very blood boil with indignation at what I have seen and heard. Then it was that I declared if ever the opportunity presented itself to defend the true rights of laboring men, and smite those who unmercifully oppressed them, I would lift up my voice and cry aloud, in the name of the God of Israel.[57]

Specifically, concerning George Pullman's official philosophy contrasted to his operative treatment of his employees, and his "operative" versus his "official" goals, Carwardine said:

In this age of rapidly increasing fortunes, when men became rich in a day by speculation, rearing a fabric of success upon the ruin of others, I am willing to accord him all honor; but when Mr. Pullman as a public man stands before the world and demands of us that we regard him as a benefactor to his race, as a true philanthropist, as one who respects his fellow men, who regards his employees with the love of a father for this children...I confess as a minister of the gospel, delivering my message in the shadow of these deserted shops, I fail utterly to see the point. The facts are not in accordance with the assertions made.[58]

Carwardine hardly saw George Pullman's model town as an enlightened attempt to harness a science of humanity toward the betterment of society. Rather, he identified the operative goals, the real intent, to be class centered and self seeking. Speaking of the model town, he said:

It is the most un-American town in all America. It belongs to the map of Europe. It is a civilized relic of old world serfdom. Today we behold the lamentable and logical outcome of the whole system.[59]

Countering those who referred to his pro-labor position and criticism of the "captains of industry" as un-American, Carwardine countered:

He (Pullman) is the King, and he demands to the full measure of his capacity all that belongs to the insignia of royalty. It is about as difficult for an ordinary man, one of his employees, to see Mr. Pullman as for a subject of Russia to see the Czar. Every official of his company is absolutely subject to his authority..if you once dispute the will of the king, (note references to Pullman and the black employees in his Pullman cars, expressed in *Roots: the Next Generations*, ABC TV, week of February 18, 1979) off goes your head. Imperialism on part of the king, breeds imperialism in the court. Even subordinates become infected with the disease, and great harm is thereby produced among the subjects.[60]

Carwardine clearly saw a reversal in the hierarchy and meaning of values, and the manifestation at all levels of values, institutions, and sanctions as interpreted by and for the benefit of capitalist magnates. He wrote:

Whatever the fathers who organized this government intended it to be, we, their successors, have evidently drifted very far away from the original intention of the founders. It is no longer a government of equal rights for all....Capital seems to be organized to destroy the independence of labor and defeat its efforts at elevation; and labor is organized not only to protect itself, but to retaliate on capital. These conditions can not be perpetuated.[61]

Carwardine's Christian Socialism

Carwardine, in his sermons and writings, emphasized that his purpose was to help, in his way, "to stir the heart of this whole nation until the 'white slaves' of industrial tyranny be emancipated...." He referred to his position as "applied Christianity," applied to humanity; "the gospel of mutual recognition, of co-operation, of the 'brotherhood of humanity.'" He condemned the "rabid and capitalistic press," which was so permeated with the twisted American values manifested in persons such as Pullman that the public remained ignorant of the real facts and prejudiced toward those persons most American in their actions.

Unlike Pullman, and unlike many corporate leaders today, who want the government to stay out of the management of the economy and regulation, to keep their "hands off" (laissez-faire) so that the noble capitalist trustees could care for everyone's needs, Carwardine encouraged government regulation. He was also realistic enough to realize the necessity to "play the game" of power politics, to organize and get important and powerful people on your side.

It is interesting to note Carwardine's reaction, when Commissioner Wright, during the U.S. Strike Commission hearings in July, 1894, asked him if he carried his views far enough to advocate what was known as "state socialism" as a solution to the difficulties. Wright reminded Carwardine that he had been charged with being both a socialist and an anarchist. It is interesting that Commissioner Wright and Carwardine agreed that it would be difficult to be an anarchist and a socialist at the same time. Carwardine, responding to Wright, said he was not prepared to take the position of "state socialism" as a solution to the difficulties, "as of yet." However, he said, "...I confess I am inclined very much toward some of these things."[62]

Carwardine went on to say that the polarity, the dividing of status quo defenders and opponents into "true americans" and "anarchists" was most fortunate. He said the charge of anarchism was so low that he really didn't like answering it. However, he said, he could be what one might call a "Christian socialist."

It is interesting that Carwardine was most willing to identify himself as a Christian socialist, but less willing to identify with state socialism. He said:

To suppose for a moment that I, who am American born, my father a soldier who died for his country - to suppose that I for one moment would be thought an anarchist is to me one of the most contemptible and false charges that could possibly be brought against me. I might be what you would call a Christian socialist, but as to anarchy, I repudiate it entirely.[63]

Carwardine's Christian socialism left no room for violence as a method of implementation. "Ballots not bullets are the things that win in this country.... A government of the people, for the people and by the people. Free schools - free speech - free press - free homes - free government."[64]

It appears here that Carwardine, like many Christian socialists, remained rather naive and did not see the real implications of his societal critique. On the other hand, in the midst of the Pullman Strike, when bullets did speak loudly as did other forms of coercion, remembering the fate of the Haymarket riot participants and how the captains' of industry influence reached into all spheres of society, government, churches, schools, media, etc., Carwardine questioned the wisdom of identifying with state socialism and the impact that would have on the Pullman workers' cause.

Addressing the Federated Trades Council in Green Bay, Wisconsin, Carwardine denounced trusts, corporations, and monopolies, and advocated the co-operative commonwealth, joint proprietorship, profit-sharing, and a condition of society based on the principles of the "Sermon on the Mount." (Matthew 5-7, Luke 6:30-49 in the New Testament) There is an element of idealism here. Just what are the implications of the Sermon on the Mount for a pragmatic program; and what about the problem of implementing programs that represent the morality of a particular religious persuasion in a society that is so heterogeneous, with so many persuasions, and commitment to keep separate church and state?

Carwardine also encouraged organization as necessary to play the power politics game, especially when capital continued to pool its interests and business was well organized. Business organizations bribed legislatures and influenced courts, so labor must apply pressure on behalf of its interests.

Carwardine, on several occasions, tried to make clear the source, motivation, and criteria for his Christian socialism. He viewed Jesus Christ as the greatest political economist the world had ever known. The ideals of the Christian state, he said, were the ideals of the truly just society. The social revolution that was in process, exemplified in the Pullman Strike, was leavened by Christianity and was the "new coming of the kingdom of God." Christian socialism, he felt, was the only kind of socialism that could really help the workingman, socialism that was founded on the golden rule and the Sermon on the Mount.

In an address he gave in Sioux City, Iowa, on March 31, 1898, he made what he felt were careful distinctions between his "Christian socialism" and other socialistic tendencies of his day. He said he was afraid of the socialism founded upon the teachings of Karl Marx rather than Jesus Christ, which appealed to many workmen. Marx's socialism, to Carwardine, was a materialistic socialism, and would lead to, if implemented, "inane dead levelism." "Such a condition may be pleasant to dream about - a Utopia for the enthusiast, but such a condition will never be realized in this hard work-a-day world with human nature full of aspiration and activity."[65]

Carwardine had a problem here. On the one hand he desired to cling to the Protestant work ethic and its antipathy to "inane dead levelism" while on the other hand he abhorred the twisted, self-interested use of the Protestant ethic in the hands of the captains of industry. On the one hand he wanted to reconfirm his commitment to "Americanism" whatever that might mean, but on the other he wanted to attack the reversal and reinterpretation of meaning given American values. On the one hand, he affirmed his "Americanism" and his basic acceptance of free enterprise, being afraid that the loss of free enterprise would cause a loss of individual aspiration. But on the other hand, laissez-faire capitalism did not give that equal opportunity to achieve and express individual aspiration.

Therefore, he constantly separated himself from the Marxian socialism, and recommended what he called the "socialism of the Sermon on the Mount," which encouraged the "love of neighbor as one's self." The problem here, of course, is the problem cited throughout our discussion of Christian socialism, and that is the problem of translating such general, idealistic phrases as the "socialism of the Sermon on the Mount" into actual programs and policies concerning resource distribution.

It is one thing to say Jesus Christ was a great political economist, who espoused various social, moral, and economic teachings; it is another to define just what this means in the realm of resource distribution programs and policies. Certainly the "Christian community" lacks consensus on just what this means!

It is interesting, when we discuss the idealism of Carwardine and the difficulty of translating his Christian socialism into specific programs and policies, to see that one of his main criticisms of Eugene Debs and other socialists was their unrealistic idealism. He admired Deb's sincerity, but concerning his idealism Carwardine wrote:

> He is so much in advance of what can be the popular
> judgment, so far as methods are concerned, that he is unable
> to accomplish all that he has hoped. His sympathies are quick
> and profound, but he allows them to make him impracticable,
> in my judgment, and they lead him into declarations and acts
> which I fear do not help the cause. What is needed at this
> time is good hard practical sense instead of inflammable

agitation. I admire Debs for what he wants to do, but question some of the ways by which he wants to do it.[66]

He criticized another Christian socialist, the Rev. F. L. Herron of Grinnell, Iowa, as also being too much of an impractical dreamer.

He is another man who is a dreamer, but a lovable personage. He wants to accomplish a tremendous good in the world, but he seeks to establish at this time a condition which will be possible only when the millennium shall have arrived. We have to deal with things as they are, and not as we would wish them to be. Mr. Herron's 'Christian commonwealth' is a beautiful conception, but we of today must do the work which is close at hand, and not attempt to establish now these conditions which, if possible at all, can come only to future generations and centuries.[67]

Carwardine has at this point excellent advice to those who recognize that if the social sciences are to be applied to human society, as Comte suggested many moons ago, they must be value-laden to the hilt. However, this value-ladenness must not cause the appliers to become so idealistic and so much dreamers, or so self righteous in a sense of correctness, that one becomes incapable of seeing "things as they are" instead of "things as one would wish them to be."

How often we fail to attempt, as W. I. Thomas suggested, to "define the situation" as the subjects of our research do, but instead impose our preconceived definition of the situation. We then become incapable of facilitating an intelligent and possible transition from one point to another.

It would be good at this point to summarize some of the implications for action that Carwardine saw in his thought. Carwardine believed that Christian socialists should not endeavor to destroy American society or American capitalism, but put capitalism behind the Constitution where it was meant to be, and not ahead of the Constitution where it was in practice. He rebelled against the reversal in the hierarchy of American values that characterized laissez-faire capitalism in the late 19th and 20th centuries. He abhorred the fact that property rights had superseded human rights and demanded that the situation be corrected. He knew there were certain ways in which reform could be implemented, and for his basic orientation, rationale, and methodology he turned to the Social Gospel, Populism, and other Christian socialists and developed his own version of Christian socialism. Some of his recommendations for reform, nebulous though they be, were: government had to take a more active role in regulation and move toward more public co-operation, ownership, and direct political involvement; and the relationship between labor and management, government and the governed, and all human concerns, had to be based on the principle of the "golden rule" and the ethics of the Sermon on the Mount.

Carwardine did take further steps in his endeavor to implement Christian socialism via "evolutionary" rather than "revolutionary" means. He wrote regular newspaper columns, went on lecture tours, and was nominated by the Prohibition Party (it must be remembered that the Prohibition Party was one of those involved in the Populist coalition) and ran as its candidate for the Illinois legislature in the 27th district. Although he lost the election, he did endeavor to direct his Christian socialism and Populism into a political party that was supported by the church, labor, and other Populist-oriented groups. Therefore, one of Carwardine's cardinal beliefs was that Christian socialists, if they were to implement their goals, had to work "with the system", and "within the system", and must, through legislation and political office, try to bring about "evolutionary" rather than "revolutionary" change, and that meant using "ballots" rather than "bullets." This much is clear in Carwardine's Christian socialism, though other specific programs and policies for production and distribution are unclear.

In concluding this section on Carwardine's Christian socialism, the article in the *Chicago Fireman's Journal*, endorsing Carwardine's candidacy and encouraging others to vote for him, is appropriate:

> His record proves that at all times, in all places, he had the welfare, the betterment, the happiness of the common people at heart. His ringing denunciation of the unscrupulous acts of corporate power have had the effect of correcting abuses which had existed for years. His labors in behalf of the firemen of this city are still fresh in the minds of people. His forceful articles in the *Chicago Examiner*, which were served to the readers of that great journal every morning for breakfast, awakened the people of Chicago to a realization that they were permitting a system to exist which would disgrace the hardest taskmaster of ante-bellum days. The articles in the *Examiner* and *American* informed the people of Chicago....[68]

Carwardine's Christian socialism, and its expression through his Pullman Strike activities, book, preaching, lecture tours, newspaper articles, and his endeavor to win a seat in the legislature, found frequent expression and sympathetic ears.

ENDNOTES

[1]Carl N. Degler, *The Age of the Economic Revolution 1876 - 1900* (Glenview, Illinois: Scott, Foresman and Co., 1967), p. 125.

[2]*Ibid.* p. 130.

[3]*Ibid.*, p. 124.

[4]H. Shelton Smith, Robert T. Handy, and Lefferts A. Loetscher, *American Christianity: an Historical Interpretation with Representative Documents*, Vol. II: 1820 - 1960 (New York: Charles Scribner's Sons, 1963), p. 359.

[5]*Ibid.*, p. 362.

[6]Degler, p. 127.

[7]Donald B. Cole, *Handbook of American History* (New York: Harcourt, Brace and World, Inc., 1968), p. 178-181.

[8]Ibid., p. 162, 168.

[9]Norman Pollack, "Populism: Realistic Radicalism," *Conflict or Consensus*, p. 99.

[10]*Ibid.*, p. 94.

[11]*Ibid.*

[12]Letters between William H. Carwardine and Henry Demarest Lloyd. Deposited with Wisconsin Historical Society, Henry Demarest Lloyd Correspondence, 1894 - 96, 1906 - 07, Boxes 4, 5, 6, 14. 1894 - February, 1895, Box 4, letter from Carwardine to Lloyd, July 6, 1894.

[13]*Ibid.*, Carwardine to Lloyd, August 3, 1894.

[14]*Ibid.*, Carwardine to Lloyd, December 28, 1894.

[15]*Ibid.*

[16]*Ibid.*, Lloyd to Carwardine, January 1, 1895.

[17]*Ibid.*, March - December, 1895, Box 5. Carwardine to Lloyd, August 29, 1895.

[18]*Ibid.*, Lloyd to Carwardine, September 3, 1895.

[19]*Ibid.*, Carwardine to Lloyd, September 10, 1895.

[20]*Ibid.*, January - August, 1896, Box 6. Carwardine to Lloyd, April 21, 1896.

[21]*Ibid.*, Lloyd to Carwardine, April 25, 1896.

[22]Ibid., 1905 - 1907, Box 14. Carwardine to Mrs. C. L. Withington, May 5, 1906.

[23]Pollack, p. 97.

[24]*Ibid.*

[25]"Industrial Problems, Rev. Mr. Carwardine's Eloquent Address," *Toledo Commercial*, February 23, 1897.

[26]"Millionaires and their Abuses of Opportunities," *Toledo Daily Blade*, February 23, 1897.

94

[27]*Ibid.*

[28]William H. Carwardine, address to graduating class of summer school, LaSalle, Illinois. June 24, 1896.

[29]"Liberty Enlightening the World: an Able Address to Workingmen by Rev. W. H. Carwardine, the 'Pullman Divine,'" *The Daily Northwestern* (Oshkosh), September 11, 1897.

[30]*Ibid.*

[31]*Ibid.*

[32]*Toledo Commercial*, February 23, 1897.

[33]*Toledo Daily Blade*, February 23, 1897.

[34]Charles Kingsley," *The New Columbia Encyclopedia* (N.Y.: Columbia University Press), 1975, p. 1481.

[35]"Saint-Simon, Claude Henri de Rouvroy, comte de, *The New Columbia Encyclopedia* (N.Y.: Columbia University Press), 1975, p. 2402.

[36]Peter d'A. Jones, *The Christian Socialist Revival 1877 - 1914* (Princeton, New Jersey: Princeton University Press, 1968), p. 7.

[37]*Ibid.*, p. 79.

[38]*Ibid.*, p. 86, 87.

[39]*Ibid.*, p. 160, 161

[40]*Ibid.*, p. 161.

[41] Dombrowski, James. The Early Days of Christian *Socialism in America.* (New York: Octagon Books, Inc., 1966), p. 26.

[42]*Ibid.*

[43]George Herron, "The Social System and the Christian Conscience," *The Kingdom*, (August 18, 1898).

[44]Dombrowski, p. 189, 190.

[45]George Herron, *The New Redemption* (New York, 1893), p. 15.

[46]Dombrowski, p. 59.

[47]*Ibid.*, p. 100.

[48]*Ibid.*, p. 104.

[49]*Ibid.*, p. 131.

[50]*Ibid.*

[51]Jones, p. 241.

[52]*Ibid.*

[53]*Christian Socialist*, III, No. 36 (May, 1886), p. 190.

[54]*Christian Socialist*, VII, No. 76 (Sept., 1889), pp. 135 - 136; VIII, No. 81 (Feb., 1890), p. 29.

[55] Jones, p. 337.

[56] *Ibid.*, p. 407

[57] William H. Carwardine, *The Pullman Strike* (Chicago: Charles H. Kerr and Co., 1894), p. 111.

[58] *Chicago Herald*, May 21, 1894.

[59] *Ibid.*

[60] Carwardine, *The Pullman Strike*, p. 49.

[61] *Ibid.*, p. 122, 123.

[62] *United States Strike Commission Report on the Chicago Strike of June - July, 1894.* Senate Executive Document No. 7. 53rd Congress, 3rd Session. (Washington D.C.: Government Printing Office, 1895), p. 448.

[63] *Ibid.*, p. 449.

[64] "The Great Industrial Problem." *Evening Advocate* (Green Bay). March 26, 1897.

[65] "For The cause of Labor." *Sioux City Journal*, March 31, 1898.

[66] *Ibid.*

[67] *Ibid.*

[68] *Chicago Fireman's Journal.*

CHAPTER IV
CARWARDINE AND THE PULLMAN STRIKE
A CLASH OF VALUE SYSTEMS

This chapter presents a general description of the causes, issues, and procedure of the strike followed by a detailed discussion of Carwardine's particular role. His book, *The Pullman Strike*, written in the midst of the crisis, left no question as to who was responsible for the strike. The basic problem was the inhumanity with which corporations dealt with labor. Carwardine, after speaking of this inhumanity, wrote:

> I do not and never have hesitated to place the responsibility of the strike upon the Company. The public must bear in mind that while the action of the employees seemed hasty, still they had great cause for action. To say that it was produced entirely by the 'labor agitator' is to insult the intelligence of the finest body of mechanics gathered together in any one place in the United States. I contend that when a body of men such as we have here, lay down their tools and leave the work bench, as did these men, that they are actuated by some great underlying motive, and that it will not do to call them idiots and fools. These employees were in a very sensitive and suspicious state of mind. A long winter, with its countless causes for grievance and dissatisfaction, was just behind them.

They had been so ground between the upper mill stone of 'low
wages' and the nether mill stone of 'high rents', the continued
oppression of the 'straw bosses', the smothered but still
unsuppressed dislike of the general and local management,
which has added to rather than sought to alleviate their
troubles, and a system of surveillance that seems to be
indigenous to the very atmosphere of the place, that they were
in no condition to be trifled with by the Company.[1]

The employing class had come to view the labor unions as a
challenge to its power. Therefore it opposed the unions, and used any
means it could to destroy them. An important factor in the Pullman strike
was the refusal by the employers to recognize the local unions and the
American Railway Union, and the refusal to bargain collectively with them.

Most of the nation's populace had been bombarded with the
employers' view of labor unions, through their control of the major opinion-
making forces such as the press, schools, and churches. "The newspapers
have printed, the teachers have taught, and the clergymen have preached,
in the main, the capitalist side of the struggle," was the view of many labor
sympathizers.[2]

Employers attempted to deal directly with their workers, rather than
work through unions, and formed managerial unions to exert their power.
These "employer associations" gave a united front in opposition to labor
unions and their demands. Some of the coercive methods used by
employers against workers were the "iron-clad oath" (yellow-dog contract)
where the worker had to promise that he would not join a union under
penalty of losing his job; discrimination against and discharge of known
unionists; black listing, where employer spies reported on organizing efforts
among workers so they could be destroyed and the "undesirable workers"'
names were passed on to other employers who would then refuse them

work; conversion of some workers into "company policy" armed for possible use against strikers; and the use of courts.

The United States Congress in 1890 passed the Sherman Antitrust Act. Instead of being used against the trusts, it was more often implemented as an "antilabor act." For example, the Sherman Antitrust Act, from 1892 to 1896, had the following results in the courts. There were 5 cases brought against trusts. One of these cases was won, four were lost. The "batting average" against the trusts was .200. Five cases were brought against labor. Four of these cases were won, one lost, for an average of .800.[3] The Sherman Act, applied against the Pullman strikers, was one of the victorious antilabor cases.

George Pullman, as already noted, had built the town of Pullman as a business venture and a solution to labor problems. Carwardine in *The Pullman Strike* said that from August, 1892, to August, 1893, the Pullman shops saw a good degree of prosperity and activity. Work was abundant, wages were fair, and the force of employees increased to between five and six thousand persons. Then came the great financial panic in 1893 and the ensuing depression. Labor unemployment and dissatisfaction was brought to a peak. The stranglehold of laissez faire philosophy on the nation and the modification of traditional values could be seen in the action, or better, the inaction of the federal government. Businessmen and statesmen alike viewed dips in the business cycle as unfortunate, inexplicable interruptions in prosperity for which there was no governmental remedy. When President Cleveland called Congress into a special session, the only anti-depression recommendation he proposed was the repeal of the Sherman Silver Purchase Act of 1890.

When the panic and depression worsened, each political party blamed the other. Labor said the blame lay with capitalist greed. Others blamed

Wall Street's "dark, mysterious, crafty, wicked, rapacious and tyrannical power [attempting to] rob and oppress and enslave the people."[4]

In reality, the causes of the crash were many. There was a decline in railroad construction; a reduction in the number of orders for rails, steel, and machinery; a depressed agriculture; European investors, confronted with their own financial panic, began to withdraw invested capital from the United States; and many other reasons.

The immediate problem, as far as the Pullman workers were concerned, was that within one year they were confronted by 5 wage cuts, accompanied by no corresponding reduction in the rents charged for company houses and utilities. Other problems were also present, and could be considered under the term paternalism. Richard T. Ely, writing for *Harper's Magazine* in 1884, said of Pullman's company town, that though admittedly a probably enlightened attempt to deal with the peculiar problems of labor, "the conclusion is unavoidable that the ideal of Pullman is un-American. It is not the American ideal. It is benevolent, well-wishing feudalism, which desires the happiness of the people but in such a way as shall please the authorities." Ely quoted one worker to have said that "we are born in a Pullman house, fed from a Pullman shop, taught in the Pullman school, catechized in the Pullman church, and when we die we shall be buried in the Pullman cemetery and go to a Pullman hell."[5]

Carwardine wrote that in the winter of 1893-94, the cutting of wages and administrative abuse of the workers were atrocious. Mutterings of dissatisfaction were constant. "There will be trouble in the spring" was an expression he heard often among workers throughout the winter. Destitution, want and suffering were common. "As a pastor I came in contact directly with much suffering. Repeated cutting of the wages with no corresponding reduction of rent exasperated the employees. I was aware that the men were being organized into local unions."[6]

The plight of the Pullman workers attracted the attention of other workers' organizations in the Chicago area, including the newly formed American Railway Union (A.R.U.). The A.R.U. was organized under the leadership of Eugene V. Debs in June, 1893, and was an expression of his desire for a single industrial organization for all railroad workers. The previous spring before the winter crisis in Pullman, the A.R.U. had won a great victory against J.J. Hill's formidable Great Northern Railroad in a strike that lasted only 18 days. In the spring of 1894 the A.R.U. formed in Pullman a shop-wide union of locals organized by departments. By May, 1894, about 35% of the Pullman workers were union members. A general committee (later called the Central Strike Committee) of forty-six men was elected to negotiate for the Union and, if necessary, to declare a strike. It is significant that the local unions in Pullman had taken the initiative to approach the A.R.U., having heard of its success, and having been in search of someone to champion their cause. They therefore appealed to Mr. Debs and Mr. Howard of the A.R.U.

Meetings were held between the A.R.U. and the Pullman workers in Kensington. Debs and Howard repeatedly counseled the men not to strike, but to wait until the A.R.U. had become stronger and could assist in the redress of grievances. A committee of workers tried to obtain a hearing with Manager Middleton, but received no response. Another committee was appointed to meet with Vice-President Wickes. Wickes received the committee, listened to their grievances, and promised that Mr. Pullman would give them a final answer the following week. On the day appointed, the committee appeared and Mr. Pullman delivered to them his first statement. He refused to accede to the employees' demand for a restoration of the wage scale of 1893, on the ground that he had taken contracts for new work at a loss. As proof, he agreed to permit an inspection of the company books. He also stated that he could not reduce the rents of his houses. However, he did agree that none of the persons on the workers' committee should be discharged, and stated that their grievances should be investigated.

Carwardine said that the employees were disappointed in the results. He wrote:

> Mr. Pullman had given out that he had taken contracts for new work at a loss, because out of love for his employees he desired to keep the shops open. Unfortunately the men had never seen any evidences of paternal love on the part of Mr. Pullman in his previous dealings with them, and they could not disabuse their minds of the thought that perhaps he was keeping the shops open, and taking work at a loss in order to get his returns in rent. Also they felt that his refusal to reduce their rents was unjust. They were suspicious and in no condition to be trifled with.[7]

It is important to note, that Carwardine said he was sure Mr. Pullman himself had no idea of the true state of affairs, and did not fully realize just how unjustly his employees had been treated. Later in the development of the strike, Carwardine repeatedly emphasized that a good deal of the problem lay in George Pullman's ignorance of the behavior of Pullman officials, foremen, and sub-bosses.

The day following the committee's meeting with George Pullman, three members of that committee were "laid off." Carwardine wrote, concerning the matter: "Cases have been cited to me of employees, who, having incurred the displeasure of those in authority, were 'laid off,' and returning again and again for work found that they were really discharged."[8] The three men who were "laid off" discovered that it was the direct result of the complaints they had made to the management concerning abusive treatment by certain superintendents. The superintendents retaliated by issuing the lay offs. The whole committee resented this action as a violation of Mr. Pullman's agreement with them. They also resented the fact that Pullman's promise of an investigation of grievances had been carried out, but by a carefully selected committee of strongly pro-management persons. The workers felt that no one acted for their defense, to see that their side was fairly represented. Their grievances were made light of and treated as trivial and inconsequential.

Therefore, on the same night of these events, the employees met in a secret all-night session composed of about forty-six men representing the various local unions. They voted unanimously to strike the following Saturday. There seems to have been a "spy" in their midst, because their deliberations and decision reached the ears of the company early Friday morning. They went to work at 7 a.m., but by 9 a.m. the leaders of the strike committee were informed through their own spies that the management knew of their strike plans and had decided to lock up the shops at noon on Friday. The workers, not wanting a lock-out, passed the word to each other that they would beat the lock-out by first walking out themselves. This they did. Carwardine, commenting on the development, said: "About six hundred remained until the noon hour, a few returned until the evening, when notices were posed on the shop gates to the effect that the shops would be closed indefinitely and the works closed down. Thus began the great Pullman strike."[9]

It was on May 11, 1894, that the Pullman workers' grievance committee requested that the workers strike. Although Eugene Debs of the A.R.U. believed the timing was wrong, he believed the strikers' cause was justified. Wages were far below subsistence level and the employees were becoming more deeply in debt to the company. On May 16, Debs let his feelings be known to the strikers when he said of George Pullman:

I believe a rich plunderer like Pullman is a greater felon than a poor thief, and it has become no small part of the duty of this organization to strip the mask of hypocrisy from the pretended philanthropist and show him to the world as an oppressor of labor . . . If it is a fact that after working for George M. Pullman for years you appear two weeks after your work stops, ragged and hungry, it only emphasizes the charge I made before this community, and Pullman stands before you as a self confessed robber . . . The paternalism of Pullman is the same as the interest of a slave holder in his human chattels. You are striking to avert slavery and degradation.[10]

It was at this time that Carwardine became actively involved. He had been in Pullman as pastor of the First Methodist Episcopal Church for two years when the strike broke out. He did not encourage the calling of a strike, but he, like Debs, felt it was justified due to the conditions in the town. On Sunday, May 20, 1894, he preached a famous sermon, using for his text Luke 10:7, "The laborer is worthy of his hire." In this sermon, which will be treated in detail later, Carwardine said George Pullman refused to give adequate assistance to his employees during the panic of 1893 and its ensuing destitution. While many workers and their families were in great need, Pullman pretended there was no destitution. "To the casual visitor it [the Pullman system] is a veritable paradise; but it is a hollow mockery, a sham, an institution girdled with red tape, and as a solution of the labor problem most unsatisfactory.[11]

During the depression, and especially in the winter of 1893-94, said Carwardine, Pullman refused to lower the quarterly dividends to stockholders, or to reduce his salary or that of the highest officials, the town authorities, and the straw bosses. However, he ordered a cut of 33-1/3% and more in workers' wages and refused to lower the house, water and gas rents. He reduced many workers to the verge of starvation and severe hardship. The company town, he said, "is the most un-American town in all America. It belongs to the map of Europe. It is a civilized relic of old world serfdom. Today we behold the lamentable and logical outcome of the whole system."[12]

Carwardine insisted that it was the right and the duty of clergymen to speak on such subjects from the pulpit. He would not speak of George Pullman as a philanthropist or a benefactor while he manifested such behavior in Pullman. Besides his refusal to reduce workers' rents or stockholders' dividends, he continued to charge exorbitant rents from the churches, gave minimal assistance to the Y.M.C.A., and never offered an emergency hospital so badly needed in Pullman. The Pullman Company officials permitted only a partial investigation of grievances and allowed members of the grievance committee from the workmen to be discharged. Carwardine ended his vigorous sermon by telling the workers: "I am with you to the end. I hope you will get your just demands. I shall always in the future count it as the proudest moment of my life that I could say a word of comfort at this crisis, and take my stand beside you in this great and apparently unequal contest."[13]

As a result of this sermon, Carwardine received much publicity and public support from across the country. He began to give a series of lectures, aimed at middle-class audiences, to church, labor, and civic organizations. He pleaded the strikers' cause, emphasizing to the public that the Pullman workers were not simply illiterate trouble makers, but were responsible and skilled Americans subjected to intolerable conditions. In July of 1894 he expanded his cause into a book, *The Pullman Strike*. The purpose of the book was to reach the class of people who were so prejudiced against the strikers.

Meanwhile, the American Railway Union held its convention in Chicago in June of 1894. Debs and other union leaders wanted to avoid a boycott and use negotiation. A committee of six delegates and six Pullman strikers was sent to the Pullman management but was refused arbitration. The management absolutely refused to listen to any suggestions from the A.R.U. "We have nothing to arbitrate!" was the answer.

A notice was then given to the management from the A.R.U. on June 20 which said that unless the Pullman Palace Car Company adjusted the grievances before June 26, 1894, union members would refuse to handle Pullman cars and equipment, while workers in the Pullman shops at St. Louis, Missouri and Ludlow, Kentucky would be called out on a strike.

The company ignored the notice, and was strongly supported by the General Managers Association (G.M.A.). This association was a voluntary and unincorporated association organized in 1886 by 24 railroads which centered or terminated in Chicago. The members tried to establish common policies on issues of mutual interest, but at first was mainly a consultative body. After 1893, however, it strengthened its structure and formed committees to aid railroads during strikes and encourage uniform wage scales. The association felt itself challenged by the A.R.U.'s proposed boycott, and opposed it. The G.M.A. and the Pullman Company thus supported each other although there was no formal connection between the two. The association directed the activities and protected the interests of the railroads when the boycott was called.

When the G.M.A. stated that its participating managements had agreed to dismiss any switchmen who boycotted Pullman cars and refused to allow the cars to be detached from their trains, the A.R.U. struck against the railroads, and by the end of June, 1894, almost all railroad workers on the roads west of Chicago were on strike, and many lines were paralyzed. Some 20,000 railroad men were on strike in and around Chicago. The economic effects of the strike were eventually felt in 27 states, and aroused the concern of the federal government, especially Attorney General Richard Olney. Federal officers in Chicago were instructed to be alert for activities which might require federal intervention. The A.R.U. knew from past experience that an interruption in the movement of mail might easily bring intervention, so for quite a long period of time, the strikers were well disciplined, and the mail moved unhampered. Carwardine commented, that from the 11th of May until the time he wrote his book on July 23, the Pullman strike had been a remarkable exhibition of orderliness and good behavior. Up to the evening of July 5th, in the seventh week of the strike, not the slightest unusual infringement of the law had taken place. Carwardine was quite relieved over this, and called it a "model strike." For seven weeks, he said, the town was quieter than at any other time in its history, as the strikers endeavored to prove they were not "rabble." The strike leaders consistently declared that order would be positively enforced. "So determined were the men that the property of the Company should not be molested that they offered to place a cordon of men around the shops to protect them."[14]

The General Managers Association, meanwhile, appealed directly to the federal government to intervene with armed troops in order to end the strike. Lawyers representing the railroads persuaded President Cleveland and Attorney General Olney that such intervention was justified because the Pullman strike obstructed the delivery of the United States mail. Thus the attempt was made to apply the Sherman Antitrust Act as an antilabor act.

The lawyers chosen to deal with the struggle caused accusations of injustice. On June 28, 1894, Attorney General Olney appointed Edwin Walker, who was affiliated with the General Managers Association as one of its lawyers, as special attorney and counsel for the national government. Clarence Darrow, an important reform figure of the period, complained bitterly of this act. "The government might with as good grace have appointed the attorney for the American Railway Union to represent the United States."[15]

Walker was the main person responsible for the sending of federal troops into Pullman. This lent itself well to the argument of many Populist-oriented critics such as Carwardine, who had often said that monopoly interests and the federal government were in conspiracy against the interests of labor. Walker served both of his "clients" well, the government and the G.M.A. On his advice as special counsel, federal troops were sent to Pullman. He also appeared before courts on behalf of the G.M.A.'s interests, and convinced the judges that the Pullman strike and boycott were an unlawful conspiracy in violation of the Sherman Act.

Walker requested that the judges issue an injunction prohibiting officials of the A.R.U. from interfering in any way with trains engaged in interstate commerce, and prohibiting them from compelling or persuading railway workers to leave their jobs. The court responded with a "blanket injunction", which covered practically everything that Debs and other union members might do. It prohibited almost every activity the strikers had available to make a strike work. Even peaceful picketing was declared a crime. All of these prohibitions were based on the Sherman Antitrust Act, an act supposedly passed to curb the trust.

Debs and other union leaders proceeded with their work in spite of the injunction. In the middle of July they were arrested for contempt of court. The backbone of the strike was thus broken. The Pullman Company, the G.M.A., the government, and the courts had combined to win another victory for the "capitalists." Many of the railway companies and the Pullman Company refused to take back some of the strikers, and others they hired on their own severe terms.

It was the arrest of Debs for contempt of court that concerned Carwardine when writing to Henry Demarest Lloyd in a letter discussed earlier. Carwardine sympathized with Debs' cause, and stated so. Attorney General Olney directed the argument before the Supreme Court in March of 1895 when Debs and his friends made an unsuccessful appeal concerning their contempt sentence. Debs was put in jail for six months (May through November, 1895). It was after this that Debs joined the Socialist movement and served as its presidential candidate for several elections.

Many things happened, however, between the government's injunction and the trial of Debs and other union leaders. Governor John P. Altgeld of Illinois argued against federal intervention, but to no avail. Attorney General Olney secured the injunction against the union and on July 4, President Cleveland sent some 2000 federal troops to Chicago to enforce the injunction and protect the mail. When the troops arrived, so did confusion and violence, and the union lost control of the situation. Mobs destroyed cars, burned and stole property. Twelve people were killed while many more were arrested. None or few of the Pullman strikers were in the mobs.

Carwardine explained how violence broke out. On the evening of July 5, when the A.R.U.'s boycott against Pullman cars was at its peak, the Illinois Central Railway decided to run the mail train known as the "Diamond Special." There was some difficulty at the Kensington depot, and the train was stopped. Later in the evening, a mob of "hoodlums and fellows of the baser sort", arriving from South Chicago, set fire to a number of Illinois Central Freight cars about a mile north of Pullman. The next morning a mob of the same character gathered at Kensington, marched past Pullman on the railroad track and overturned box cars. A United States deputy by the name of Stark fired wildly into the crowd. William Anslyn, an innocent spectator about 250 feet from the scene, was shot. Carwardine then described the scene: "Falling upon his face, he endeavored to rise, when Stark, according to the deposition of eye witnesses, advanced and deliberately fired a shot into the back of the prostrate man. Two days thereafter Anslyn died, as the result of the brutal deed. The deputy is still at large."[16]

The mob was infuriated by this deed and tried to lay their hands on Stark, but were stopped by the police. Passions rose and the air was filled with threats and rumors. In the afternoon of the same day more cars were set on fire. In the evening the federal troops restored order.

The *Pullman Review* on July 14, 1894, printed an article concerning Mr. Anslyn's funeral. It is interesting that while Carwardine referred to Stark as a United States deputy, the newspaper called him a detective of the Michigan Central Railroad. One of the major complaints of the strikers and their defenders was that such "double duties", between being a railway management detective and a federal deputy were common. The article stated that about 1,000 persons attended the funeral services, and Carwardine gave a short address on the deceased. The emphasis of the article was that the shooting was a deplorable affair, and that Anslyn was a foreman of an industrious and honorable nature. The various "patriotic" organizations of which he was a member were listed, obviously a response to the usual claim that Anslyn, as others associated with the Pullman strike, were subversive, un-American, and anarchistic. The federal injunction was to be the key factor in ending the effectiveness of the strike. It was a swift and deadly weapon, and from the Pullman strike on, it came to be used with frequency and great effectiveness by managerial interests who desired to break strikes. The employer could simply go to the federal or state courts and persuade the judges that if they did not restrain the strikers, great harm would be done to tangible and intangible property; tangible property such as factories, machinery, and material, and intangible property such as the right to do business, the good will of the public toward the employer and his product, and the right to make a profit. Judges could be easily persuaded, and were deluged with calls for injunctions against all sorts of matters: against strikers parading, picketing, assembling near places where strikes were in process, distributing pamphlets, and even attending church services or praying and singing on public highways.[17] Labor was to spend many years agitating for a law that would limit the use of injunctions in labor disputes.

Judge P. S. Grosscup of the federal district court, and Judge William A. Woods of the United States circuit court, issued the injunction against the leadership of the Pullman strike and boycott. The injunction was a blanket injunction in that it could be interpreted so broadly and used against so many activities. The injunction was to prevent any person from "directing, inciting, encouraging, or instructing any persons whatsoever to interfere with the business or affairs, directly or indirectly" of the railway companies.[18] To again illustrate the strong hold big business had on the government and the courts, Judge Grosscup remarked privately that he opposed such employment of the judiciary in labor disputes because it was partisan action.[19] Many Populist-oriented state governors rebuked President Cleveland for sending federal troops. Illinois' Governor Altgeld was furious, and said he would have asked for federal troops if he had felt it necessary. He and other governors, such as William Stone of Missouri, Davis Waite of Colorado, James Hogg of Texas, Sylvester Pennoyer of Oregon, and Lorenzo Lewelling of Kansas, found federal intervention in their states objectionable, and attacked the process of "centralization" which was impinging upon local rights.

Carwardine believed that the presence of federal troops and the martial law they represented had a demoralizing effect upon the community and that local authorities could have kept order. The Central Strike Committee, composed of members from each of the local unions, with

Mr. Heathcote as the chairman, had worked hard to keep radicalism at a minimum. The committee along with the local authorities would have been sufficient, and certainly would have enhanced the morale of the workers, since in essence, matters would have been solved by local and not outside forces.

Carwardine praised Heathcote and his committee for their concern to retain orderliness. He also praised the Pullman Strikers' Relief Fund, headed by a committee of ladies interested in the cause of labor. They made appeals to the public on behalf of the needy strikers, and aroused considerable sympathy and aid. They disbursed money and provisions. Carwardine wrote: "To summarize, the total amount of money not including provisions given to the Relief Fund up to July 21st, 1984, was $15,000.00, the total expenses to same date, $14,000.00 . . . In the distribution of provisions, the greatest care has been taken to see that justice is equally dispensed to all. At this writing 2,700 families are being provided for, counting six to a family."[20]

He said there had always been class distinctions in Pullman, but the strike intensified them. Outside of the great mass of employees and their families, there was a little coterie of individuals termed, in the evening paper, the *Chicago Evening Post*, the "aristocratic element", whose headquarters was the Florence Hotel. There the officials and the elite of the community assembled and discussed the situation. They were, of course, against the strikers who they believed were un-American and subversive. Just as in today's society, these self-righteous patriots put on their lapels, to offset the arm bands of the subversive strikers, little American flags. Carwardine, just as critics today, resented the flag being taken from those whom he believed were expressing true Americanism in meaningful dissent and being placed on the chest of the oppressors. He wrote:

Soon after the white ribbons were donned by the striking employees and their sympathizers as suggested by Mr. Debs, those who were opposed to the strike wore a miniature American flag. Does this mean that they who wore the flag indicate thereby that the striking employees are un-American endorsers of lawlessness and anarchy? Does it mean that the Pullman strikers are treasonable in their attitude of a quiet and determined demand for justice and a fair wage? Let it be remembered that no corresponding town of its size in the country can boast of more well organized, active, patriotic societies than the town of Pullman, - the F.A.R., the P.O.S. of A., the P.O.D. of A., the Sons of Veterans, etc. There is as much if not more patriotic fervor for the old flag and American institutions to the square inch in Pullman than in any other town in the country.[21]

One sees here evidence of the all pervading belief in America's organic progression toward providential greatness, based upon that vital essence incorporated in the terms nature, providence, and will. Carwardine and other reformers were as compelled as the managerial interests to prove that they were indeed consistent with America's essential greatness. He wrote, that "if any one class more than another was entitled to wear and carry the American flag, it was the workingman.[22] These reformers were not denouncing Americanism, but that distorted version of Americanism as embodied in laissez faire economics.

Carwardine was a renegade as far as the majority of American clergy were concerned. During the Pullman strike, many ministers throughout the country condemned Debs and the American Railway Union. They saw the strike as a threat to social stability and believed the men behind it should be punished. For example, the Rev. John A. B. Wilson of the Eighteenth

Street Methodist Episcopal Church in New York City, on Sunday, July 8,
preaching on the theme, "The Strike and Its Terrors," blamed Debs for the
turmoil and declared him a demagogue, "the son of a saloon keeper, a man
reared and educated upon the proceeds of human ruin . . . This is the man
who is able to bring death to hundreds, ruin to thousands and starvation to
hundred of thousands."[23] Typical of those defending the status quo he saw
no fault in the system that laissez faire capitalism had created.

The Rev. A. B. Leonard, who was a general missionary of the
Methodist Episcopal Church, preached on July 8 at Staten Island, New
York, and called for the imprisonment of Debs and Illinois' Governor John
Altgeld as enemies of society. On the same day Dr. Herrick Johnson,
professor at the Presbyterian Theological Seminary in Chicago, preached in
Brooklyn, New York, and said:

> There is but one way to deal with these troubles now and that
> is by violence . . . The time has come when forbearance has
> ceased to be a virtue. There must be some shooting, men
> must be killed, and then there will be an end of this defiance
> of law and destruction of property. Violence must be met by
> violence. The soldier must use his gun. He must shoot to
> kill.[24]

Here is a beautiful example of the sanctity with which the right of
property was held and the degree to which traditional values had been
distorted. It is also a vivid example of how the text of the Christian gospel
which says, "love your neighbor," and how the person of the compassionate
Christ, are so often twisted and distorted by the "established" when it thinks
that law and order and its position are threatened. It shows how vicious
"providence on behalf of the haves" can be.

It is interesting to note the early response of fellow preachers to
Carwardine's work in the strike. It was a response of condemnation. He

spoke out in the face of a hesitant and unsympathetic press, while church leaders were generally timid, uncertain, skeptical and critical of his approach. In the appointment of pastors, he was penalized by his annual conference of the Methodist Episcopal Church by an appointment to a "minor charge" (in the rhetoric of ministerial concern for status) behind the Chicago Stock Yards. When the fervency of emotions and the threat of the strike had passed, and when the church began to reconsider his role, he was more "favorably" appointed and praised by the Chicago Preacher's Meeting.

A telling article appeared in the *Northwestern Christian Advocate* for September 19, 1894. The *Advocate* was an official paper of the Methodist Episcopal Church, published in Chicago and edited by the Rev. Arthur Edwards. In an editorial, the writer said that those labor leaders were in error who said the workingman was neglected by the church. He pointed to Carwardine as an example of a responsible pastor who insisted that the rights of workmen should be respected, but who also was not responsible for mistakes made in the heat of word and action. The Chicago Preacher's Meeting, the writer pointed out, had recently met and supported Carwardine in his stand and had expressed a hope that workingmen would see the church as true to its tradition and a friend of the "industrious and aspiring men who aimed to support his family, be a useful citizen and serve God."[25]

The writer of this editorial reflected many phenomena. He obviously found it easier to speak when the heat was off, was concerned for stability and lack of conflict, accepted the basic values of laissez faire capitalism, felt a sense of guilt or public pressure for its lack of action, and offered an apology for the behavior of the church during the labor crises. He offered an explanation for the delay in expression of concern by many pastors when he said: "Concrete issues, suddenly presented, may find good men momentarily at a loss, and time may be needed for due digestion of the elements concerned. However, that very deliberation is born of desire to be exactly just and wisely executive.[26]

Most preachers, like the general public, accepted the modified values of the time, and feared conflict which threatened natural organic progress, stability, and personal position. This could be seen in the Chicago Preacher's Meeting of September, 1894, when in congratulating Carwardine, it was still emphasized that, "it should be remembered that whatever violence may have been mingled with that very broad war known as the 'Pullman Strike', Pullman strikers did little violence, while our church members in Pullman have clean, peaceful, and blameless hands. To Mr. Carwardine very much of this may justly be credited."[27]

Up to this point, the discussion has centered upon general issues involved in the Pullman strike, the context within which Carwardine acted, and the response to his actions. It is time to deal with specifics. A rather detailed discussion will be presented concerning Carwardine's activities and motivations during the strike. He was extremely critical of the Pullman management, their policies, actions, explanations for those actions, and their twisting of events as given to the communication media. There is a great amount of material concerning the position and reactions of the Pullman management. However, certain lines had to be drawn for this study. Since our concern is primarily Carwardine and his role, only those statements and actions of the management which directly apply to him will be presented. However, the bibliography lists many materials published by the management, and readers desiring to read further in this area may find these references useful.

As stated earlier, there was a division among the Pullman ministers concerning the strike. In the spring of 1894, the Rev. E. C. Oggel of the Greenstone Memorial Church preached a eulogy for George Pullman. He told the "Horatio Alger" story of Pullman's rise from rags to riches, and his well-deserved fame and fortune of the day. The town of Pullman, he said, was an experiment in "contemplated beauty and harmony, health, comfort, and contentment."[28] He condemned the union leaders as agitators, and said to the workers in his congregation, on the verge of starvation, "half a load was better than none."[29] It is significant, that the attendance at Oggel's church declined in the next few weeks, and he went on a vacation from which he never returned.

At the same time that Oggel was eulogizing Pullman, Carwardine was preaching the gospel of "applied Christianity." He recognized that "the relation existing between a man's body and soul are such that you can make very little headway appealing to the soul of a thoroughly live and healthy man if he be starving for food."[30]

The May 14 issue of the *Chicago Daily News* carried an article quoting various Pullman pastors and their attitudes toward the strike. The writer of the article said, referring to Rev. Oggel:

> The Presbyterian minister over in the beautiful green-stone
> church on Watt avenue -the swell street of the town - threw
> a barrel of cold water on the strike saying it was ill-advised,
> precipitated by outsiders and would not win public sympathy,
> because it was insufficiently justified either by low wages or
> improper treatment.[31]

Oggel predicted that the strike would fail, that there was no reasonable hope for success. By this time he did, however, profess sympathy for the men and hoped the outcome would be "better than he anticipated."

The Rev. McGrath of the Episcopal Church made no reference to the strike during his church services, but in private said all he cared to say was that he very much deplored the "unfortunate occurrence."

Father Tinan of the Roman Catholic Church counseled the men at this morning service to do no violence and preserve good order. Unlike

Carwardine, he felt it was not the business of the church to interfere in business matters. "My congregation is mostly composed of the men who have quit work and their families. The policy of our church is to keep out of any business affairs and abstain from comment on anything of the nature of a strike. So I have merely advised the men to keep the peace."[32]

The Rev. Fred Berry, the Baptist preacher, devoted half the evening service to the strike, but dealt almost altogether in generalities.

Perhaps of all the ministers in Pullman the Rev. Carwardine of the Methodist Church, said the writer, stood nearest the people. He quoted Carwardine:

> I refrained from any comment on the situation Sunday, but next Sunday I shall perhaps deliver a sermon directly to the point. I sympathize with the men and want to see them win the strike. The movement may have been a little premature, but the men have had their grievances. I think Mr. Pullman is an honest and truthful man, but I believe he has been ill-advised. His published statement I believe was truthfully made, but there are many circumstances which have contributed to this demonstration.[33]

Carwardine did deliver that sermon the following Sunday, May 20, 1894. The sermon was extremely important because it launched him fully into the struggle. Not only did the workers rally behind him, but the Pullman Company reacted, and the newspapers spread his sermon far and wide. Soon he was being asked to make speeches in many places. This sermon was a key event in Carwardine's life.

Before analyzing the sermon, something should be said about a very impressionable event in Carwardine's childhood that certainly was a factor in his Populist-oriented, social gospel concern manifested from the pulpit. He described the evening in his book, *The Pullman Strike*.

I well remember, when an orphan boy in the city of New York, having to work for six years under an abusive foreman in the composing room of the New York Evening Post. Of all the men I have ever met, he was the embodiment of tyranny, a man of considerable ability, but foul in language and despotic in authority, the daily terror of all who were under his influence. He treated men like dogs, swore at them and abused them without stint. In those days there was engendered in my soul a hatred against tyrannical foremen and abusive treatment of men which has never left me, and which during the past months of our long and sad winter, made my very blood boil with indignation at what I have seen and heard. Then it was that I declared if ever the opportunity presented itself to defend the true rights of laboring men, and smite those who unmercifully oppressed them, I would lift up my voice and cry aloud, in the name of the God of Israel.[34]

On the day before Carwardine gave his great sermon, the *Chicago Times* carried an interesting article concerning the intimidation he faced. The article noted that he had addressed the Pullman strikers in terms by no means flattering to the Pullman Company, and that he planned to preach the next day in the same vein on the subject of the strike, "under the very eaves of the deserted factory." It was a matter of common knowledge, read the article, that this pastor had been warned, if not threatened, that his fearless course would alienate the friendship of the Pullman Company and perhaps bring serious disaster on himself and his church. "So much for the Pullman boast that no intimidation is practiced in Pullman." The article went on to say: "But if Mr. Carwardine has the courage of his convictions and is a true follower of the gospel he professes he will speak the truth that is in him and thereby gain a reward which no Pullman bulldozing can destroy."[35]

Carwardine did have the courage to deliver his sermon, and indeed, the response to it gave him further courage to become even more deeply involved in the labor cause. He drew strength from the unexpected support. In his book written in July, he said: "When I delivered my sermon on 'The Pullman Strike', ten days after its employees walked out of the shops, I had no idea that it would have created the interest that it has."[36] However, it was because of that interest that his book, *The Pullman Strike*, was written.

Many newspapers throughout the country carried accounts of the sermon. One of the most complete accounts was that found in the *Chicago Herald* for May 21, 1894. The headlines over the account read, "Preacher to Strikers, Pullman Minister's Plain Words; Rev. W. H. Carwardine, of the Methodist Church, asks Some Pointed Questions of the Magnate, Who, He says, is Unworthy of Praise Sometimes Given." Carwardine's text for the sermon was Luke 10:7, "The laborer is worthy of his hire." After referring to the strike among the workmen as the main question of the hour, he said it was his duty as a minister of the gospel to look the situation squarely in the face, without equivocation. His conscience would not allow him to remain silent. He referred to the words of Rev. Oggel the previous Sunday, and wished him a pleasant journey to "the land where strikes are unknown and the poor always submit to the lords of the soil," and begged him "to think on us occasionally while we eat the half loaf that is better than no bread."

Carwardine assured his congregation that his conscience was clear, and thanked them for their expression of hearty sympathy. However, he recognized that many persons were filled with fear that the company would retaliate for their stand, and said:

You need not fear that the company will retaliate upon us as a church for anything I may say. It dare not in the face of public opinion. And, let me add, if the fears of some of you should ever be realized, better a thousand times that our church be disorganized by the company than that we truckle to them, forego the God-given and American right to free speech, smother our convictions, muzzle our mouths, fawn beneath the smiles of any rich man or corporation. Better to die for the truth than be surfeited by a lie.[37]

Here is an excellent manifestation of Carwardine's labor, Populist, social gospel, and Christian socialist orientation.

He went on to say a few words regarding Mr. Pullman himself. He refused to say anything about Pullman that savored of "fulsome eulogy or nauseating praise." "I will not speak of him as a philanthropist, for I have never seen nor heard of any evidence of this. I will not speak of his services to his age, because I know of none. I will not refer to his services to his country, as history is silent thereon."

Carwardine admitted that George Pullman had great business ability, having raised himself from a poor boy in a country town to his present position. However, having recognized his business ability, and the values of the age which condoned what he had done, Carwardine did not agree with the very distorted values he manifested. Again Carwardine's Populist orientation was clear when he said:

In this age of rapidly increasing fortunes, when men became rich in a day by speculation, rearing a fabric of success upon the ruin of others, I am willing to accord him all honor; but when Mr. Pullman as a public man stands before the world and demands of us that we regard him as a benefactor to his face, as a true philanthropist, as one who respects his fellow men, who regards his employees with the love of a father for his children and would have us classify him with such men as George Peabody, Peter Cooper and George W. Childs, I confess as a minister of the gospel, delivering my message in the shadow of these deserted shops, I fail utterly to see the point. The facts are not in accordance with the assertions made.[38]

Carwardine said that if Pullman were the benefactor he claimed to be, let him answer a few questions. Though not a financier, Carwardine thought he knew right from wrong. "Why does not Mr. Pullman stand before his directors and demand of them, upon the basis of morality and right, that, instead of declaring a quarterly dividend of 2 per cent in these terribly depressed times, they be content with 1½ percent and place the $114,000 representing the other one-half per cent to the credit of the payroll?"

He also asked why Mr. Pullman did not, when he demanded a cut of $33^1/_3$ per cent and more in the wages of his employees, which upon careful investigation he would have found would reduce them to severe hardship and many to the verge of starvation, also reduce the high rents and water taxes levied upon the same employees? When he reduced the wages of his employees, why did he not reduce his own salary and those of all his higher officials, local management and town officials, heads of departments, foremen and straw bosses? When he cut the price of labor in his great freight car shops from $14 a car with one inspector, to $7 a car and three inspectors, why did he not get along with two fewer inspectors and spread their wages over his already reduced pay roll? Why did Mr. Pullman, in the midst of a hard winter, when the hours of work were few and the wages at their lowest ebb; when whole families were in want; when the churches were burdened with their heavy rents and were at the same time seeking to relieve the poor; when the Woman's Relief Union was doing all it could to help the destitute; why did Mr. Pullman not heed the cries for help, and why did he and his company give little to alleviate the poor conditions? In view of these questions Carwardine posed to Pullman, we may observe that George Pullman manifested the distorted values of the time, where property rights had superseded human rights in the hierarchy of values.

A question which Carwardine raised in his sermon and emphasized in his book, was, why did Pullman permit one of his officials to publish a statement that there was no destitution in Pullman, and that there could not be as long as $720,000 was deposited in the bank to the credit of the laboring men, a statement which Carwardine had reason to believe was, in effect, false and misleading? This matter will be discussed when Carwardine's book is analyzed, but the issue was that the $720,000 deposited represented deposits for executives, foremen, outside depositors, and others and was not only that of the men on strike.

Carwardine said that the wages paid to the Pullman workers were an insult:

I am told that the average wages paid by the company is $1.87 a day. I doubt it much. It is claimed that the men are not receiving 'starvation wages'. I know many of which this is true, but they are the exception and not the rule. I know a man who has had, after paying $14.50 rent for four small rooms and 71 cents for water rent, but 76 cents a day left to feed and clothe his wife and children. When we remember that this is an average case, that it is on the basis of full time, then in the name of all that is just and right, I say God help that man if his dependents be many or if sickness invade his home. And I cry 'shame' upon the rich corporation that dares to insult the

American workingman with such a wage as that. No, no; it is wrong! Eternally wrong![39]

Carwardine said that throughout the country, great factory chimneys rose like church steeples. However, if in the future justice were not meted out to the laborer and capital were not less tyrannical, those "temples of labor" would be turned into the slaughterhouses of anarchy and the music of the hammer and anvil would become discordant with the raging elements of infuriated conflicts. So it was that he vividly set forth the seriousness of the situation if changes were not made. Carwardine never encouraged "slaughter or anarchy," but he saw it as understandable and inevitable if conditions continued to oppose the worker as they had.

Referring again to the local strike, he said that "the great trouble with this whole Pullman system is that it is not what it pretends to be. To a casual visitor it is a veritable paradise; but it is a hollow mockery, a sham, an institution girdled with red tape, and is a solution of the labor problem most unsatisfactory."

Why, asked Carwardine, did Mr. Pullman not do something for the moral and educational development of the community? Why did he extort such exorbitant rents from the churches? Why did he not assist the Young Men's Christian Association just a little? Why did he not give an emergency hospital, which was so badly needed? Probably the underlying complaint of Carwardine toward George Pullman, whom he considered largely ignorant of the baseness of the town's problems, was his physical absence from the town which increased his ignorance. "And, last but not least, why, let me ask does he not as a man of flesh and blood like ourselves, bring himself into a little closer contact with the public life of our town, cheer his employees with his fatherly presence and allow the calloused hand of labor occasionally to grasp the gentle hand of the man who professes to be so intensely interested in our welfare?"

Carwardine said that until Mr. Pullman could give a satisfactory answer to these many questions, he would not consider him a benefactor to his race, a philanthropist, or one who had done anything for prosperity which would cause mankind, when Pullman died, to rise up and call him blessed.

A plea that accurately illustrated Carwardine's Populist-oriented applied Christianity, was this:

> Thou eternal God, what poison has crept into human nature and the spirit of true democratic simplicity that can cause this man who himself was once a poor mechanic at the bench, but who is now a pampered millionaire, entrenched behind his gold, to deny these just requests of those whose hands have made him rich, and to heed not the tears of wives and children who have been simply existing upon the crumbs which fall from the rich man's table![40]

Carwardine ended his sermon with a powerful analysis of Pullman, and said the town's orientation, not the workers, was un-American. It was the town, not the workers, that was subversive to the essence of America's greatness, that essence which was currently mouthed but not practiced except in a distorted form. The great trouble with the town of Pullman, viewed from the standpoint of an industrial experiment, was that its deficiencies overbalanced all its beauties. "It is the most un-American town in all America. It belongs to the map of Europe. It is a civilized relic of old world serfdom. Today we behold the lamentable and logical outcome of the whole system." After an exhaustive treatment of the causes of the strike, in which he held the officials of the company to have been culpably negligent in their permission of only a partial investigation of grievances and the allowance of members from the strike committee to have been discharged, he said: "I am with you to the end. I hope you will get your just demands. I shall always in the future count it as the proudest moment of my life that I could say a word of comfort at this crisis, and take my stand beside you in this great and apparently unequal contest."[41]

All the Chicago papers did not agree on the quality of Carwardine's sermon. Many felt he was a trouble maker. The *Chicago Times*, however, admired his stand, and on May 22 stated, after an analysis of his sermon, that since George Pullman lacked mental adroitness or agility of intellect, he would probably ignore Carwardine's remarks.

Carwardine remained very outspoken. Mr. Pullman declared that he received only 3% profit from his houses, but Carwardine said that was hypocrisy. Pullman was paying taxes based on a deflated evaluation, on the value of the land when it was a swamp. At the same time he was receiving inflated rents based on the value of the land after improvements. The 3% profit figure was misleading, because it was based on the value of the land after improvement, a value upon which Pullman was not paying taxes. Carwardine also resented his congregation having to pay $480 to the company for such small and simple facilities as those in the Arcade. He had gone to the bank to get financial help, but was refused, because the banker did not approve of his stand on the strike. He was wrong about the injustice of rents and wages, the banker said; Mr. Pullman had offered to let the men look at the books, that should have settled the issue. Carwardine replied that he felt Mr. Pullman was indeed sincere in opening his books to inspection, because they had been doctored. There were double sets of books, so the inspection of the materials opened to the workers would not contain the true facts. "Of what use would it be for the men to look at the books? Ten million sets of books would not change the injustice of the state of facts."[42]

The *Chicago Times* of May 22, 1894, carried another interesting article. The writer said that Mr. Pullman ought to answer Carwardine's charges as stated in his sermon and other speeches, "if he were not such a very busy man." The article went on to say: "But it is to be feared that the eleemosynary minded gentlemen who runs the great car shops in the duchy to the south of Chicago at a loss in order to keep his beloved employees at work is too steadily engaged in clipping coupons for himself and drawing up trial balances of the company's losses for his men to give his reverend interrogator's somewhat personal queries the refuting answers he might otherwise be delighted to furnish."[43] The writer said that, due to Mr. Pullman's busy condition, the only answer Carwardine was likely to get would be an order barring him from the church or perhaps an edict expelling him from the "duchy". Again it is interesting that critics were using the same values of the time - America's unique essence and destiny -that business interests were using, to attack these interests as un-American. Referring to Pullman as a "duchy" was similar to Carwardine's calling the town a remains of old world serfdom.

This same article in the *Chicago Times* praised Carwardine for his love of truth when he attacked the Pullman system, and stated:

> True words and brave words those of the Rev. Mr. Carwardine
> and in striking contrast to the half-a-loaf presents of that other
> Pullman clergyman, Dr. Oggel. Here indeed is a preacher
> worthy of his profession. His scathing but truthful arraignment
> of George M. Pullman and his associates merits the admiration
> of every lover of truth and true courage.[44]

The strikers' response to Carwardine was favorable. One factor that seemed to enhance a favorable response was the general knowledge among the strikers that strong pressure had been brought to bear upon him to keep quiet on the subject. Miss Wood, secretary of the relief committee, said that every word Carwardine spoke concerning the company was the truth:

> We all know that he went to the officials of the company with

accounts of the suffering among the employees long before the strike, and we know that his statements were poohpoohed. Mr. Pullman knew, or should have known, there was suffering among his workmen, but he took no steps to help them. Mr. Pullman told the committee that 90 cents a day was good wages for a working girl. I get $1 a day and pay $17.71 a month rent for myself and mother. I have a brother in Montana who helps us out or we could not live. Mr. Carwardine told only the truth.[45]

One of the workers was very helpful over Carwardine's efforts that seemed to be gaining momentum. He said:

If Mr. Pullman can go along just as he is now he will be very well satisfied indeed. As long as the houses are occupied the company can keep them insured. The slow process of starvation will be the weapon employed by the Pullman company to defeat its striking employees *(sic)*, and it looks now as if a sympathetic community would interpose to defeat Mr. Pullman along the line of battle.[46]

Carwardine's book, *The Pullman Strike*, has often been mentioned. He was writing this book throughout June and July, in the midst of the strike, and the openness to his sermon and other addresses was an added incentive to have the book published. Much of the book is an expansion of points mentioned in previous sermons and addresses, with a detailed collection of illustrations as to the grievances of the strikers. Rather than summarize the whole book, which would be repetitive and extremely lengthy, key ideas and illustrations will be lifted out to augment the materials already mentioned.

The dedicatory page is important because it shows another source of Carwardine's values. The book is dedicated to his father-in-law, the Rev.

John Williams, pastor of the First Methodist Episcopal Church, Creston, Illinois, "who was for thirty years in his early life connected with the Daily Press of New York City, and who did loyal service at that time in arousing public sentiment to the needs of the toiling masses."

The introduction to the book was written by another friend, the Rev. John Merritte Driver, pastor of the First Methodist Episcopal Church in Marion, Indiana. The introduction describes why Carwardine could speak with authority concerning the strike. He was a resident of Pullman for two years, was familiar with almost every face and fireside in the town, knew George Pullman and his officials, knew Eugene Debs and his friends, and knew what both sides had done - when, how, why, and with what results. "In a sense, therefore, he knows more about the whole conflict than either Debs or Pullman. Each knows his own side only, the author of this volume knows both sides."

The purpose of the book was made quite clear, to clarify the issues, set right the facts distorted by the press and the company's statements, and break through the prejudice set against the strikers. The introduction read:

> May its plain, honest facts banish the flagrant misinformation
> with which the secular and even the religious press has been
> teeming for weeks, and may it be the mission of this book to
> stir the heart of this whole nation until the 'white slaves' of
> industrial tyranny be emancipated and receive the treatment
> becoming the sons and daughters of the Most High.[47]

Carwardine, in his introductory remarks, reminded his readers that he was doing exactly what some critics told him to do when they said, "mind your own business and preach the gospel." He was preaching the social gospel, the gospel of applied Christianity, applied to humanity; "the gospel of mutual recognition, of co-operation, of the 'brotherhood of humanity.'"

Carwardine said he was trying to show Pullman the way it really was. Most people, except for those who lived in Pullman, received their opinions through the pictures presented by Mr. Duane Doty. Doty was the editor of the *Pullman Journal,* and was also the historian and statistician of the Pullman Company. He strongly admired the principles upon which the town was based, which, added to his charm as a conversationalist, caused him to give a most delightful impression of Pullman. The first part of Carwardine's book, then, is a verbal tour of the town as he points out the various buildings and parks, discusses how they fit into the Pullman system, and how they were a part of the oppression.

His discussion of the Green Stone Church was interesting, because he criticized it from the point of view of one interested in applied Christianity, interested in having a building and a program that would serve the town's social needs. George Pullman, of course, was interested in a church for its beauty and source of moral unity and control. Carwardine's criticisms were interesting because they are identical with those of recent pastors in Pullman. The building is not suitable to a community oriented ministry. Carwardine wrote:

> As a piece of ecclesiastical architecture it is perfection from
> the outside, but for practical church purposes it is useless,
> being composed of one large room, the auditorium, and three
> small rooms at the rear. It has no separate Sunday School
> room, parlors, class room or any of the modern conveniences
> now found in churches.[48]

After guiding the reader past the buildings and parks usually shown to visitors, Carwardine went on to such sights as Fulton Street, and the great tenement blocks. These buildings were three stories high, and held from 300 to 500 persons under one roof. The tenements were divided into those of two, three, and four rooms apiece. The rooms were mostly occupied by

reigners, and though air and light was available, there was only one faucet
for each group of five families.

The brick yards were the "eyesore" of the town. Located there were
four rows of little wooden shanties, sixteen by twenty feet, consisting of a
sitting room, two bedrooms, and a kitchen in a lean-to. Carwardine said the
cabins could easily have been built for $100 apiece, and yet they were
rented for $8 a month, or $96 a year. Commenting on the town in general,
he said:

> The whole impression of the town, outside of the central part,
> is that it is crowded and unwholesome. The houses are all
> built in solid brick rows. The monotony and regularity of the
> buildings give one the impression that he is living in soldiers'
> barracks. There is no such thing as a home in the American
> sense of the word; owing to the high rents hundreds of families
> having two or three room apartments, keep boarders and
> roomers, striving in this way to add to the earnings of the head
> of the family, to make both ends meet. During the past winter
> it took the earnings of both host and boarder to pay the rent
> and keep above the plain of destitution.[49]

Carwardine described homes where there were no front doors for the
families living upstairs. Other homes were so occupied, that if one desired
to reach the family living upstairs, he was compelled, night or day, to pass
through the apartment of the family on the lower floor. Carwardine thought
that this destroyed the sanctity of the home and was not conducive to the
best morality.

Following the theme of his sermons and speeches, he declared that
the town was un-American, a sham; that a resident was made to feel, at
every turn, the presence of the corporation. He made an interesting
statement to the effect that he felt many persons remained in Pullman

because of the challenge the company posed and their determination to fight it. "It is a civilized relic of European serfdom. We all enjoy living here because there is an equality of interest, and we have a common enemy, the Company, but our daily prayer is, 'Lord, keep us from dying here.'"[50] Accompanying the problems of paternalism, low wages, and high rents were the problems of favoritism, nepotism, petty jealousy, and an all pervading feeling of insecurity. Carwardine quoted an "eminent writer in *Harper's Monthly*", who in 1884 wrote an article about Pullman. Ten years ago, said Carwardine, the same problems were evident. The town was "a species of benevolent feudalism, and as to its morals, the prevailing tendency at that day was, 'the desire to beat the company.'"[51]

Carwardine discussed his attitude toward George Pullman, and repeated much of what he had declared in his May 20th sermon. The important point is that he felt Pullman could have prevented the great strike, without harm to himself. The city, state, and federal governments had appealed to him, but he did not respond. Thousands of dollars worth of property was thus destroyed; the trade of half the nation had been paralyzed; human lives had been sacrificed and the "bloody riot hung like a pall over the city and country"; but nevertheless, Mr. Pullman fled the scene of action and refused to make even a formal concession. He would not have had to sacrifice either his dignity or his money. It was this matter of absence that Carwardine believed was so criminal.

Carwardine again made it clear that, though he did not agree with everything Eugene Debs said or did, he saw him as a champion of labor and a direct contrast to Mr. Pullman. Debs, he said, was a man of great executive ability and a wonderful organizer, as well as a powerful orator with charisma. He had an essential quality. It was not necessary that men agree on everything, but they ought to believe sincerely in that which they profess. Debs was thoroughly sincere in the cause he advocated even though he was somewhat of an "enthusiast." Carwardine said:

> I make no apology for his attitude in the matter of the 'boycott', except that he was forced by the logic of his position into his fight with the Railroad Managers. Mr. Debs needs no word from me. He is fully capable of taking care of himself. Mistaken he may have been as to his methods, but sincere he is as to the cause of labor . . . Debs has always counseled moderation, and positively demanded of his followers to commit no violence. Had all the strikers been of like mind, and had the mob elements, the rabble, and cheap foreign labor imported to his country by such gentlemen as the Railroad Managers, not taken advantage of the situation to commit violence, the condition of things would have been different.[52]

It is important to point out, that men such as Debs and Carwardine might have agreed often on goals but differed on the methods to attain goals. This is why it is so dangerous to lump all dissenters into one basket, for it ignores many points of difference between individual dissenters.

Carwardine again illustrated his applied Christianity when he warned that until the American people would recognize the true merits of the laboring man's position and demands, and until the corporations would cease to be tyrannical and millionaires to be arrogant, and until there was more of the love of God and fellow-men in the hearts of rich and poor, society would never be "rid of such men as Pullman and the mission of such as Mr. Debs." Carwardine also condemned the "rabid and capitalistic press," which was so permeated with the twisted American values manifested in persons such as Pullman, that the public remained ignorant of the real facts and prejudiced toward those persons most American in their actions.

Carwardine spent a good part of his book refuting Pullman Company statements concerning the strike. Three statements in particular were refuted, one given on May 9th by Mr. Pullman in answer to the strike committee; another given to the public on June 12th by the company just previous to the boycott on the Pullman cars by the A.R.U.; and a third given on July 13th by Mr. Pullman, in New York, defending his attitude in refusing to arbitrate. Carwardine criticized the Chicago press for the way it presented the company's statements, saying that if he had lived in Chicago instead of Pullman, and knew nothing about the strike except what he read in the leading Chicago newspapers, he would have raised his hand in holy horror against the "wicked Pullman strikers" and any person identifying with their cause. However, he said, since he did live in Pullman, and since he was independent of the company and employees, he could read between the lines of the "beautiful Pullman statements" and note the fallacies of their position.

Carwardine held Mr. Pullman responsible for the strike because of his presidency of the company and the great influence he held over the whole Pullman system. Again, consciously making Pullman appear to have been old worldly and un-American in contrast to the workers, he said of Mr. Pullman:

> He is the King, and he demands to the full measure of his
> capacity all that belongs to the insignia of royalty. It is about
> as difficult for an ordinary man, one of his employees, to see
> Mr. Pullman as for a subject of Russia to see the Czar. Every
> official of his company is absolutely subject to his authority .
> . . if you once dispute the will of the king, off goes your head.
> Imperialism on the part of the king, breeds imperialism in the
> court. Even subordinates become infected with the disease,
> and great harm is thereby produced among the subjects.[53]

As indicated in an earlier address, Carwardine felt a major cause of the strike was the unfair and tyrannical dealing on the part of certain foremen and other administrators, of which Mr. Pullman must have been aware. Why did he not see to it that these problems were remedied? Carwardine indicated that the company had its own gestapo, spies planted among the workers to follow their actions and protest deliberations. He said that information of everything that went on in the town, social, political, shop talk, town talk of any importance, was conveyed by letter every week to headquarters. He referred to the time when he was himself aroused from sleep in the middle of the night by a man employed by the company, who, in the presence of his wife, took a stenographic report of the interrogation concerning a member of his church who had had a confrontation with a Pullman worker. "I dislike espionage," said Carwardine.

It was with this frame of mind that Carwardine criticized the statement made by George Pullman in response to the strike committee. He referred to Pullman's statement that, "a little more than a year ago the shops at Pullman were in a prosperous condition; work was plenty, wages were high and the condition of the employees was indicated by the fact that the local savings bank had of savings deposits nearly $700,000, of which nearly all was the property of the employees."

Carwardine said that "a little more than a year ago" would have been about June, 1893. He presented the *Report of the Pullman Loan and Savings Bank* for July 25, 1893, as published in the *Pullman Journal*. The savings deposits amounted to $631,354.25, a difference of $68,645.75 from that quoted by Mr. Pullman. Carwardine said the question was whether or not the $631,354.25 was entirely the amount deposited by the employees, mechanics and laborers?

It is a well known fact that some of the officials are depositors in the local bank. The salaries of these gentlemen are large . . . Furthermore, the local storekeepers are depositors also. Many storekeepers in Roseland, Kensington and Gano deposit therein, also treasurers of lodges. One gentleman in the employ of the company is said to have $30,000.00 deposited . . . If all or any of this was counted as the savings of employees, then it would be comparatively easy to make such a glowing statement . . . And further, there are many working people not employed by the Pullman Company who place 'savings deposits' in the Pullman Bank because of its reliability.[54]

Carwardine also asked, if $700,000 indicated the amount actually belonging to the employees in 1893, how was it that they were in arrears, as the company elsewhere affirmed, $70,000 on rent at the time of the strike? "If the employees were worth $700,000 in August, 1893 and in May, 1894 had not only drawn it all out of the bank, but were $70,000 in arrears on rent besides, it certainly proves that their wages were so small that they were gradually moving toward the 'starvation wage' point, as affirmed so often by the employees."[55] What made the matter worse, he said, was the vast wealth of the company at the same time. It had a surplus for one year, 1892, of $3,250,389.07, with a two per cent quarterly dividend of $600,000 over and above all expenses, while the wages of its employees were viciously cut. Why, asked Carwardine, did Pullman not stand before his board of directors, who represented the 3,246 stockholders of the Pullman Company (of which 1,800 controlled the funds of educational and charitable institutions, and of which 1,494 were women, among them supposedly Queen Victoria) and demand of them, on the basis of morality and right, that instead of declaring a quarterly dividend of 2 percent in the midst of depressed times, they declare a dividend of 1½ per cent? The $114,000 representing the other ½ per cent could have been credited to the pay roll of the employees.

While the Pullman Company claims on the one hand that its whole system is purely financial, with not one ounce of real philanthropic blood flowing through its veins (which is certainly true of its non-arbitrating President), still it has caused thousands of dollars' worth of complimentary literature to be scattered abroad for these many years, throughout the country, like the above pamphlet, giving a quasi-endorsement to the alleged fact that the town is established as a solution of the industrial problem upon the basis of 'mutual recognition'.[56]

Carwardine then quoted from an editorial found in the *Daily Republican* of Springfield, Massachusetts, for July 11, 1894. The editorial pointed out similar incidents of the company's large profits in the face of vastly reduced wages, and then said:

It may be a question, therefore, for philanthropists and labor reformers to consider, whether Mr. Pullman, in view of the extraordinary profits he and his company were accumulating, was or was not morally bound to share more generously with his men in the effects of the hard times. He believes in paternalistic methods, and has put them in operation at his works to a degree not equalled anywhere else in America. What could be more in consonance with this policy than at such a time to dip back into the surplus of $4,000,000 made in the single previous year and keep up the wages of employees who are so carefully housed and otherwise looked after as so many dependents at Pullman? It may not be true in other cases, but it is certainly true of such a system of paternalism, that wage reductions can not be justified in the face of such profits as the Pullman Company exhibits.[57]

Carwardine also criticized Mr. Pullman's statement that the pay rolls for the year 1893 showed an average earning of over $600 per year for every person on the roll. Carwardine said that estimate was not based upon the earnings of mechanics and laborers alone, just as the savings deposits were not. The pay roll included the large clerical force, heads of departments, foremen, and others. Also, the earnings for 1893 included the great amount of money earned for overtime during the busy winter of 1893, when men worked day and night preparing cars for the World's Fair.

Carwardine attacked Pullman's statement that he had taken contracts for building cars at a loss so as to keep his men employed during the depressed times, and the publics' response: "How can Mr. Pullman pay the wages of 1893, while at the same time he is losing money on certain contracts for building cars?" The flaw in Pullman's statement, he said, was that the great bulk of work done in the Pullman shops was the repairing of old cars shipped in from all over the country. Sixty per cent of the work done in the shops at the time of the strike was repair work, not new work. Repair work was Pullman's own work, done by him under contract with the railroad corporations running his cars. A certain amount of the repair work was done at the expense of the railroads running the cars, and of course, the company, while it cut wages, did not repair cars for the roads at a less figure than before on account of "hard times."

Carwardine cited another example. While persons connected with the services on the Pullman Palace Cars, such as the laundry girls, had their wages cut, the prices of berths on the cars were not reduced to the general public. Carwardine drew upon quotes from Senator Sherman of Ohio, who had long been concerned over Pullman rates, and had proposed that the Pullman Company be brought within the provisions of the Interstate

Commerce Act, and that Congress enact a law requiring the company to give the public better accommodations at lower rates. Sherman said, in an interview presented in the *Inter Ocean*:

> I regard these rates as simply infamous. It is outrageous for us to be compelled to pay such high prices for such poor accommodations as we receive in our trips to and fro about the country . . . I regard the Pullman Company and the sugar trust as the most outrageous monopolies of the day. They make enormous profits, and give their patrons little or nothing in return in proportion . . . there is a way to reach the sleeping-car problem with ease through government action . . . The United States can easily control the charges for sleepers, just as the railway fares have been regulated by means of the interstate commerce law.[58]

Carwardine, of course, favored governmental regulation of such matters. He also expressed his recognition of "power politics", how it helped to have important contacts to implement justice. He said of Sherman's comments: "The same sentiments have been expressed by the Pullman strikers individually and upon the public platform. But when uttered by a United States Senator they carry with them a weight of influence far beyond that given to them by the poor wage-earner."[59]

Carwardine again attacked Mr. Pullman's offer to allow employees the privilege of inspecting his books. The books were doctored to suit the company's side, and it was thought that there was a double set of books kept by the company which would make it impossible to get the real facts. He raised a key point when he said that whether there were multiple sets of books or not, the fact that workers felt there were indicated the suspicious condition of mind engendered by the company's treatment of its employees.

Carwardine was particularly angry over Mr. Pullman's refusal to arbitrate. As the discussion of his Populist-orientation pointed out, arbitration was central to his program for reform. It will be remembered from his correspondence with Lloyd that he even intended to write a novel entitled, "Nothing to Arbitrate". He thought Mr. Pullman evaded the whole question of arbitration in his public statements, such as when he said:

> How could I, as president of the Pullman Company, consent to agree that if any body of men not concerned with the interests of the company's shareholders should as arbitrators, for any reasons seeming good to them, so decree, I would open the shops, employ workmen at wages greater than their work could be sold for and continue this ruinous policy indefinitely or be accused of a breach of faith? Who shall deny that such a question is plainly not a subject of arbitration? Is it not, then, unreasonable that the company should be asked to arbitrate whether or not it should submit such a question to arbitration?[60]

Carwardine angrily answered that it was never asked of Pullman that he consent to arbitration with the condition attached that he open his shops and employ his men at wages greater than their work could be sold for; nor was he ever asked to continue "his ruinous policy indefinitely." All that the strike committee asked of him was arbitration on the question as to whether or not there was anything to arbitrate. If his position were right, he had nothing to fear. Carwardine insisted that there definitely were issues that should have been arbitrated, such as less drastic cuts in wages, reduction of rents, equalization of wages, and reform of shop abuses.

He then proceeded in his book to discuss in detail the cutting of wages and to give many examples where the cuts caused extreme hardship. Mr. Pullman had deliberately misrepresented the requests of the workers, he said. The workers never intended, and Pullman knew it, to receive the wages of 1893 for work done at a loss. Pullman was familiar enough with the procedures of collective bargaining to know that the workers intended to ask for a certain wage level, and, when failing in that, to compromise on what they really did want. They expected the company to agree on a less severe cut in wages, say a cut of about 25 per cent rather than $33^1/_3$ per cent, accompanied by a reduction in rents and correction of shop abuses.

A major source of irritation was that the workers received two checks every two weeks, one a rent check and the other a pay check. These checks were issued at the bank. When the workers went to the bank to receive their two weeks' pay, the half month's rent was taken out and the pay check cashed. Not only was the current rent demanded, but back rent was requested when the conditions of the workers simply would not allow such payment. After deducting the rent, the men invariably had from one to six dollars or so on which to live for two weeks. That was not very much. Carwardine gave several examples of how this affected the workers. He cited one man who had a pay check of two cents after his rent was paid, and another who had seven cents, and was at the same time trying to support a widowed mother. "Another employee had 47 cents coming to him on his pay check, and then was asked if he would not apply that on his back rent. He was indignant. He replied: 'If Mr. Pullman needs that 47 cents worse than I do, let him have it.' He left it."[61]

The average cut in wages, said Carwardine, was $33^1/_3$ per cent, but in some cases there was a 40 per cent, and in many a 50 per cent, cut. Several examples were described by Carwardine, from various department, where the wages left after rent was deducted were inadequate for a family to live on.

Probably one of the worst features, in Carwardine's opinion, was that most of the work was done by piece work rather than time work, and the men were not given the opportunity to put in full-time. There were bitter complaints by the men over this matter. While wages and working time were cut, the large force of foremen, under-foremen, sub-bosses, and other officials was kept the same or increased, and their wages were not severely altered. He cited many laborers who, at the same time, worked for nine cents an hour for ten hours' work and thus earned the "glorious sum" of ninety cents per day. "Inspectors or sub-bosses were placed over little gangs of men, to see that the same quality of work was squeezed out of the already cruelly reduced employees, as they had always been doing. It was, therefore, not surprising in many cases that the wages were so low that with the high rents they could not live."[62] Carwardine said that many of the inspectors, foremen, and sub-bosses were tyrannical because of pressure put upon them to keep the costs of production down.

Referring again to the values of the time, and the compulsion of persons to demonstrate that they were "good Americans", it is interesting how many of the workers who wrote to or spoke with Carwardine about their grievances made this point quite clear. They did not appreciate being called un-American and subversive, and indeed they considered themselves to have been better Americans than the Pullman management. For example one letter to Carwardine ended with this notation: "P.S. I was born in the United States, as were my parents before me and as were their parents before them."

Carwardine pointed out how the conditions in Pullman, combined with various state laws, put some persons, women in particular, in a very serious predicament. There were many young women who worked in various departments. Before May, 1893, they were paid at the rate of twenty-two and one-half cents an hour. The wage cut reduced this amount to ten cents an hour, a cut of sixty-eight per cent. Many of these women were providing for parents and small sisters or brothers, as well as themselves. While they were earning from ten to eight cents an hour, the Illinois statutes compelled an eight-hour day for women. Therefore laws that had been passed as reform laws were now making the burden even greater for women workers, in that they could not work additional hours to earn more money.

Not only was there a great economic burden produced by the wage cuts, high rents, and repressive foremen, but there was a great psychological burden. Carwardine saw this, when he wrote: "Imagine how a workman must feel after laboring two weeks, to step up to the bank, and have either two cents, seven cents, eight cents, or forty-seven cents handed to him to keep his family on for the following two weeks. Not much 'mutual recognition' in that!"[63]

Carwardine noted that he believed Mr. Pullman and Mr. Wickes, though accepting the policy of wage cuts and stable rents, and though demanding more efficiency, desired the policy to be implemented gradually and evenly. Pullman had ordered for the process to "go slow". However, his managers "drove fast." His absence from the town, scarcely making a visit more than five or six times during the winter, worsened the situation, since he did not know the true state of affairs. Statements from every department were sent to him regularly, but they were "colored with such a roseate hue", that he believed all was well. However, Carwardine felt he should have made frequent visits, and since he did not, he was responsible for the present state of affairs. Certainly he should have at least seen to it that a policy of equalization was implemented. When the wages of the workers were cut, there should have been a cut in the salaries of the officials, the clerical force, the heads of departments, the foremen, and the inspectors. Also, he should not have allowed the great discrepancy between the degree of cuts in various departments. There was no recognition of the skill involved in various jobs. Cuts were made oblivious to such distinctions.

Carwardine ended his discussion of wage cuts and shop abuses by condemning what had become common practice, the appeal by the wealthy for government force in protecting their interests. Again his Populist orientation was manifested when he wrote, referring to oppressive wealthy businessmen:

> And these are the gentlemen who at the first alarm of violence cry to the government for military protection, fill the town on the slightest provocation with the police, and who themselves are so afraid of their mortal existence that they move about armed to the teeth, and in quick communication with the militia. O tempora! O mores![64]

George Pullman in his statement concerning rental rates, said the average rental of tenements in Pullman was at the rate of $3 per room per month, and that the renting of houses in Pullman had no relation to work in the shops. Employees could, and many did, own or rent houses outside the town, and the facilities and business places in the town were rented to employees or to others in competition with the neighboring properties. The renting business of the Pullman Company was, he said, governed by the same conditions which governed any other large owner of real estate, except that the company itself did directly some things which in Chicago were assumed by the city.

Carwardine challenged this statement. He said $3 per room was not the average rental. He quoted from Mr. Doty's book, and said there were 1,855 tenements in Pullman, though a few had been added since the book was published. Averaging five rooms to a house in relation to Pullman's rentals, the average came to $3.71 per room. Even that was a very low figure, because at least one-half of the tenements were empty in the midst of the strike, and about one-third of them had always been empty. If the average were based on the actual rents paid and the actual number of housed occupied, the rate would have been much higher than $3.00 per room. He quoted some interesting figures:

> I occupied a flat of four rooms on Watt Ave., and paid $14.50 rent; at $3.00 per room, I lost $2.50 per month. I next rented a five room cottage on Morse Ave., for $17.50; at $3.00 per room, lost $2.50 per month. I am now renting a five room cottage on the same street, but a better location for $18.50; at $3.00 per room, I am losing $3.50 per month.[65]

He also quoted a letter written by a real estate dealer in nearby Kensington, which appeared in the *Chicago Times*. The letter read:

> Kensington, Ill., July 17 - George M. Pullman, Esq., Long Branch, N.J. Sir: In the publishment of a recent interview with you it is stated that your renting department charges rents in Pullman in competition with rents in the adjoining town of Kensington, Roseland, and Gano. If you sincerely believe this to be true, it would be well for you to personally investigate, as with my six years' experience in the renting business in the said towns of Kensington, Roseland, and Gano, I know it to be a positive fact that flats and cottages containing parlor, dining room, two bedrooms and kitchen, with use of water and yard, have been and are rented for $10 and $12, for which similar accommodations you charge $16 and $18 at least. My statement, undoubtedly, will be verified at any time by other renting agents of this district.
>
> Respectfully,   Cornelius G. Boon
>
> Real estate and renting agent[66]

Carwardine went on to criticize the water and gas rates, higher than those in Chicago, and stated how ridiculous it was when Pullman was paying so little tax on the vast land that he owned. It was mentioned earlier that the land had been evaluated on its condition as swamp land, and it was on that evaluation that Pullman was paying taxes. Therefore the property brought to the city of Chicago less than one tenth of one per cent of its actual current estimated value. All Carwardine could say was, "what is the matter with the assessor?"

He managed to interject all through his book that probably the major complaint of the strikers was serious abuse on the part of foremen and other officials, combined with their damnable usage of black listing. Again comparing the company's practice to that of old world corruption, he wrote:

> This whole matter of black listing is worthy of Siberia. It is a disgrace to American labor. It is a boycott on labor. Capital complains of strikes and boycotts. I deprecate strikes, and I believe a boycott to be wrong, and a poor way to win good results for labor, but capital boycotts a man when she 'black lists' him. The black listed man can not only not get employment in all of the Pullman shops, and Pullman interests; but can not even get a recommendation of good character to another employer.[67]

Carwardine had often encouraged workers to be politically independent. Of course, his Populist connections explains some of his distrust of major political parties, but his knowledge of local political abuse was another factor. He saw how the Pullman Company used politics to their interests and how it punished those workers who would not play its political game. He described how, at the time of local elections, foremen talked to their workers to encourage the direction of their voting, and let them know what the consequences could be if they did not respond favorably. He cited an example during an aldermanic election, when an official of the company went to a foreman and gave him to understand that he was to withdraw his name as a candidate for a certain office and "would in all probability be expected to settle it within that day." The man ignored the threat, and continued to run for nomination. He lost, but in the process defeated the chances of the company's candidate, and the candidate opposed by the company was elected. In a few weeks, the independent foreman was asked to resign, though he had worked for the company for many years and was efficient. Two other employees interested in his candidacy were also asked to resign. Not only did Carwardine find this political abuse un-American and tyrannical, but it added to the constant feeling of insecurity among the workers.

He ended his book with a plea to the reader that he look for the real cause of labor discontent. He asked the reader not to cry "anarchy" and run away from the worker, and thereby leave him to the "tender mercies" of the militia and the police. Carwardine said that he too was against mobs and violence, but it was irresponsible to lump all dissenters into one big basket of anarchists. The evil, he said, lay not in the strikers nor their cause, but in the whole laissez faire value system and the distorted American tradition accompanying it, of which the Pullman system was a manifestation. Speaking like a true Populist, he said the inequalities of life as indicated in the social fabric of modern society were fearful. In some ways, it was the grandest age the world had ever seen, but yet there was something radically wrong in a society that boasted of its progress and advancement and yet permitted some to be so poor and others to be so rich. "It certainly looks as though the poor were growing poorer and the rich becoming richer."

The United States, he believed, was following in the tracks of ancient Rome, instead of learning from her failures. No country, he said, could prosper, and no government could long perpetuate itself and its institutions, if it did not administer judgment and justice alike to all of its people. Populism at its best was expressed in his words:

Whatever the fathers who organized this government intended it to be, we, their successors, have evidently drifted very far away from the original intention of the founders. It is no longer a government of equal rights for all. The present strike may be overcome by federal bayonets and bullets, but the trouble will not end here. There is deep unrest in the lowest strata of society, the real burden-bearers of our country, which augurs ill for capitalistic oppression in the future. The United States is to be the theater for the presentation of the best possible results of human government. We are giving an object lesson in government to the world. And these results are to be developed within a very few years, too. I therefore deprecate . . . the use of federal troops in this strike as a precedent pregnant with evil in years to come. Capital seems to be organized to destroy the independence of labor and defeat its efforts at elevation; and labor is organized not only to protect itself but to retaliate on capital. These conditions can not be perpetuated.[68]

Carwardine then made suggestions, coming out of his Populist orientation, to prevent the perpetuation of conflict. He suggested that there be "National and State Courts of Arbitration," the former in cases of appeal, reviewing the decisions of the latter, and having final jurisdiction in all cases whether of review or original. If international disputes could be settled through courts of arbitration, then he believed labor disputes could be also. He believed the "strong arm of the law" should compel the autocratic millionaire as well as the dependent mechanic to submit his case and abide by the decision. If, as in the Pullman strike, there were an obstinate refusal to arbitrate, then the federal or state governments should take possession of the railroads, the telegraph, the coal mines, or the manufacturing plants, and run them in the interest of the whole people, and not in the interest of obstinate corporations. The public good and the peace of the country, said Carwardine, demanded this.

He reversed the opposition's argument that the reformers were "subversive." He said subversiveness was not so easily associated with whole groups, but must rather be associated with individuals who may be found in many groups. For example, he said, the man or body of men, corporation or labor union, which refused to arbitrate their differences, were traitors to their country's best interests, violators of her laws, instigators to riot, and enemies of every principle that was good and pure and holy and peaceable.[69]

Carwardine's final appeal, still consistent with his value orientation, was that the laboring classes always use their ballots correctly.

It is the God-given privilege of every American citizen, purchased at the sacrifice of blood, tears and property, and which is the birthright of 4,000 years of slow and painful evolution from degradation, slavery and tyranny to the liberty of this latter nineteenth century . . . the greatest gift given by God to man outside of his blessed Son, our Lord and Savior Jesus Christ, and one that can give us, if we use it right, the grandest type of government under the sun![70]

Carwardine warned, however, that the worker must always vote on the basis of principle, not party, and vote for men who were patriots and able to represent their best interests. Again, emphasizing that the movement he represented was absolutely American, he said to the workmen of America: "Love your country. There is no better in this world. Love and uphold our constitution, and ever protect the flag for which our fathers, my father, died."[71]

Finally, he made it clear as to the purpose of his book, when he said of it:

> May you reach the homes of wealth, and awaken them to their duty, may you fire the hearts of reformers to greater deeds, may you stir the minds of legislators to the need of better laws, and may you, above all, help to bring the great mass of the laboring millions to realize that the secret of their greatest happiness and the settlement of all our industrial troubles lies in the upholding of the true principles of that Christianity, irrespective of creed, which was given to the world by Him who not only said, 'do unto others as ye would that they should do unto you', but also that 'the laborer is worthy of his hire'.[72]

In this final quotation, and in the values expressed throughout *The Pullman Strike*, one can see the influences of, and the manifestation of, the three concerns woven through Carwardine's life, labor, the social gospel, and Populism.

He received a tremendous response from his book, favorable and unfavorable, from many interest groups and many parts of the country. Labor's response was very favorable, of course. Eugene Debs wrote Carwardine a letter and said:

> It does me good to receive your encouragement, and I thank you for it. You know that I feel that the poor and labor have been neglected by the churches, and this is the reason for my keen appreciation of your friendship, for you have suffered persecution and realize with what the poor have to contend. Not until the powers which at present control our legislation, national and state, are eradicated, however, will such as you and I be allowed to rest.[73]

Carwardine received a letter from John W. Howe, secretary of Union No. 164 of the A.R.U. in Dubuque, Iowa, a letter similar to those from many labor leaders. It stated that Carwardine's sermon and other addresses had been read at union meetings, and a motion was made and passed that a vote of thanks be taken and communicated to him for his stand on behalf of labor.

It is interesting to read the *Report on the Chicago Strike of June-July, 1894, by the United States Strike Commission*. In the midst of the Pullman strike, President Cleveland appointed a United States Commission to investigate its causes and conduct. Over 100 witnesses were examined, Carwardine among them, and the committee's report included a large portion of his testimony and part of his book. The report was submitted to President Cleveland in November of 1894 and was then passed on to Congress. The commission did not place responsibility for the violence on the strikers, but on the American people in general and on the government for not adequately controlling monopolies and corporations and for its failure to protect the right of labor and to correct its wrongs. It recognized that traditional values had been distorted and the hierarchy of values altered. The commission defended labor's right to organize and even stressed the importance to society of strongly organized unions.

Persons interested in delving into the Pullman strike ought to read the commission's report in its entirety. Here, it is adequate to summarize the report. There were statements by George Pullman and his second vice-president, T. H. Wickes. Wickes was in direct charge during the strike, so Pullman had him prepare a statement covering "all the ground of the controversy." Pullman gave a testimony as to the general policy of the company, a rationale for the model community, and repeated the statements that Carwardine had challenged in his book.

Wickes discussed the various testimonies of pro-labor witnesses, including Carwardine's, and tried to show how they had distorted the facts. He cited several examples from Carwardine's book, and showed how, compared to his own records, they were incorrect. However, Carwardine had already spoken to the fallacy of referring to company records, because they were doctored and intentionally misleading, through figuring the average rents on all homes, even those not occupied, and by many other methods. Therefore, when one reads the commission report, he is confronted by a "cold war" between pro-labor and pro-management ideologies. Let it be enough to say that Wickes challenged Carwardine's book, while Carwardine challenged Wickes' basis for doing so. We are mainly concerned with Carwardine's value orientation and there are a few statements within the report that are significant in illustrating his labor, social gospel, Populist orientation.

Carwardine mentioned in his testimony that he had talked with Mr. Heathcoate, president of the Central Strike Committee, and had asked for an opportunity to speak with the committee. He encouraged the committee to seek, through arbitration, an end to the strike. He and committee representatives went to see Debs, and presented their proposal. Debs responded:

> We are about to do that very thing tonight. I meet the
> federated labor union at 8 o'clock, and we will propose a plan
> by which if the railroad managers will take back the men
> without prejudice, excepting those who have indulged in
> lawlessness, we will declare the boycott.[74]

Carwardine said at that time he felt good, because he felt he had at least done a little something. However, that same night, when representatives approached the railroad managers, they refused to have anything to do with the proposal.

Carwardine said, as far as solutions to the labor problem were concerned, he was very much inclined toward courts of arbitration. He was also inclined to be sympathetic with the idea of putting the railroads into the hands of the government, an important Populist principle. There would always be critics, he said, who would see such programs as utopian, because they would not look at the fundamental problems of their society. He had assured the strike committee, that no matter what critics might say, and no matter what the final outcome of new programs might be, "there will never come a settlement of these difficulties until employers are more just toward their employees than has been illustrated in this affair through which we have just passed. There will have to be more justice, more of the spirit of co-operation, more of the spirit of recognition.[75]

Commissioner Wright, questioning Carwardine, then asked if he carried his views far enough to advocate what was known as "state socialism" as a solution to the difficulties. Carwardine said he was not prepared to take that position, that he had not advocated it as yet. "I do not like to commit myself to the policy as yet, but I confess I am inclined very much toward some of these things."

Wright reminded him that he had been charged with being both a socialist and an anarchist. They both agreed that a man could not be an anarchist and a socialist at the same time. Carwardine then replied to Wright's question, as to how much truth there was in the public charge that he was an anarchist. The polarity, the dividing of status quo defenders and opponents into "true Americans" and "anarchists" irritated him, and he responded that the charge of anarchism was so low that he really didn't feel like answering it. However, he said, he could be what one might call, a "Christian socialist." Again one sees the coming together of labor, social gospel, and Populist values under the term, "Christian socialism." Carwardine said:

To suppose for a moment that I, who am American born, my father a soldier who died for his country - to suppose that I for one moment would be thought an anarchist is to be one of the most contemptible and false charges that could possibly be brought against me. I might be what you would call a Christian socialist, but as to anarchy, I repudiate it entirely.[76]

The conclusion of Carwardine's testimony was very interesting. He attempted to show that in spite of what Pullman or Wickes might have said, or quoted the record to have said, the situation in Pullman was tyrannical and reminiscent of European serfdom. He said that at the time of his testimony, there were about sixty-four families who had their names on a list for eviction due to non-payment of back rent, and his own name headed the list. He knew he was out of the company's grace, but, rather than publicly evict a person who practiced his right of dissent, the company preferred to make it appear as a simple business matter. The commissioner asked Carwardine if what he said were just heresay, and he answered, "no; I have reason to believe it is a fact." The commissioner then asked if there were a representative of the Pullman Palace Car Company present who desired to cross-examine Carwardine. There was no response.

Carwardine was not evicted from his home. It appears that if there had been such an eviction list, its publicity as a means to punish dissenters caused its withdrawal.

After his famous May sermon, and the publication of his book, Carwardine remained active on behalf of the workers' cause, through newspaper articles, speeches, tracts, and other means. He came to be in great demand as a speaker. His main concern was to demonstrate that the Pullman workers and others with a similar cause, were not just troublemakers. They were responsible Americans who opposed the distorted American values and intolerable conditions under which they lived. Before many church, labor, and civic organizations, Carwardine combined materials from his sermon and book into powerful criticisms of American laissez faire capitalism and the society it produced. A local newspaper in one community where he delivered his address, entitled its summary, "Methodist Clergyman, Familiar with all the Facts, Tears the Mask from St. George."

The introductions given to Carwardine when he spoke illustrate his Populist orientation. For example on July 22, 1894, he addressed a mass meeting held at Congress Hall in Chicago. He was introduced as "a friend of labor, and so was every man who was a citizen of the United States." There were some powerful implications here, to the effect that those persons who were not friends of labor were not really American citizens, but citizens of the old world feudal period. Carwardine was identified as one who believed there had been too much legislation for the rich and hoped the time would come when the laboring classes would control the legislation of the entire state for the benefit of all.[77]

The *Religious Philosophical Journal* of Chicago, for September, 1894, stated that the Pullman strike would go down in history as the turning point in the struggle for wealth which was the curse of the nation, if not of the age. Carwardine was a key figure in this critical turn of events, and his book "should be in the hands of all those interested in social matters."[78]

At another rally, Carwardine warned his listeners that the labor question was not yet settled, and for that reason he feared for the country. He loved the American flag as all true Americans did, but he would rather wear the white ribbon with the American flag on top of it; that was a sign that the strikers desired to get only what belonged to them.

He made another attempt, recorded in the *Chicago Herald* for August 6, 1894, to end the strike. He proposed that the Pullman Company remit the rent that had been piling up on its employees since May 1 and take all men back who had behaved themselves during the strike. The men would go back to work at the wage scale they had struck against last May. His program had not yet been approved by labor leaders, but it was believed that his influence with the strike committee was such that he could convince it that it was to the workers' best interests to abandon the strike and go to work at the reduced rate of wages, instead of staying out and seeing their jobs filled by new men. The Pullman Company would not lose much by cancelling back accounts; indeed the act would not be a very generous one. However, it would sound big and the publicity it would bring might be appealing to the company. The hard fact was, stated the article, the company would only be giving away a lot of bad accounts it could never collect anyway.[79]

The writer of the article displayed a bit of pessimism concerning the future of Carwardine's proposal, because the company's "secret agents" had told Mr. Pullman that one of the topics most earnestly discussed at strike headquarters was how to get back into the shops and organize another big strike just when the company needed workmen most. This pessimism proved to have been well founded, because the company's response was, "nothing to arbitrate."

In another address given in August, 1894, Carwardine gave an excellent rationale for his "applied Christianity" program. Ministers were obligated, he said, to discuss the great questions of social, moral, and economic interest. "He who denies the right of the clergy to discuss these matters of great public concern has either been brought up under a government totally foreign to the free atmosphere of American institutions, or else he has failed utterly to comprehend the spirit of the age in which he lives."[80]

On August 26, 1894, he spoke at the Hyde Park Methodist Church in Hyde Park, Illinois, near Pullman. His text was: "In the world ye shall have tribulation; about be of good cheer, I have overcome the world."

(John 16:33) Drawing again upon his Populist and social gospel orientation, he said the text gave the worker three main thoughts: there was a conflict, be encouraged, and expect victory, because Christ had fought the same battle, and had won. Therefore they ought to have hope, because they were waging a conflict with already essentially defeated foes.

On September 10, 1894, the Methodist ministers of Chicago held their regular meeting in the First Methodist Episcopal Church at Clark and Washington streets. One of the principal topics for discussion was the accusation made several times against Carwardine that he was an anarchist. It is significant that this meeting was held after the most passionate stage of the strike was over, because the attitude of the clergy was mellowing. There was a definite feeling that Carwardine and persons of his kind had accomplished a great deal, even though there was not as yet a great deal of new legislation or improvement of conditions. The accomplishment was in terms of altered public attitudes. One clergyman present said he could mention the names of many wealthy people who had told him they no longer entertained the same old views with which the capitalists looked upon labor. This sentiment, he said, was growing day by day. "I think the utterances of clergymen like Mr. Carwardine have done much to cause such a feeling for the cause of the people to become so widespread, reaching the foundations of the fabric which has hitherto bitterly opposed any advance being made by what was termed the lower class of society."[81]

It is interesting that this body of clergymen, earlier very critical of Carwardine and his activities, now passed the following resolution adopted by a rising vote:

Whereas, the Rev. W. H. Carwardine, pastor of the Pullman Methodist Episcopal Church, has been accused of anarchy in the Christian sympathy which he has extended to the working people in their recent distresses; therefore, resolved, that we, the members of the Methodist preachers' meeting of Chicago, express our utmost confidence in the Rev. Carwardine's loyalty to Americanism, Methodism, and Christianity in the manly sympathy which he has manifested in word and deed for the law-abiding working people of Pullman, and believe that the accusations of anarchism made against him have been unjust and untrue, if not malicious.[82]

Carwardine, not missing an opportunity, proceeded to read a paper on the "Problem of Labor", in which he expressed the same views which had given occasion to the accusation of anarchism, but views which now appeared to meet with the approval of the assembly.

The Rev. J. P. Brushingham of the Fulton Street Methodist Episcopal Church, said that the more "liberal" clergy would favorably consider such thinking as that expressed by Carwardine, others would not. He personally admired Carwardine, and said he considered the accusation of anarchy to have been absurd. Modern teaching should have brought persons above such accusation. He said:

Utterances which would have been classed as anarchistic or even heretic years ago are not considered such by modern teachers of the faith, no matter what their creed. The ministry of today is becoming concerned in the interests of the masses. Clergymen formerly considered themselves as belonging to a privileged class, but now take an entirely different view of the industrial question. I consider all clergymen are laboringmen-workingmen, just as much so as the man who earns his bread by labor of any kind, no matter how humble the occupation. Ministers of today are obliged to consider these questions and must speak their convictions in spite of what the pew says. It is true a small minority of the ministry is inclined to favor the wealthy class, but even the wealthy class is beginning to recognize the rights of the masses and dares not treat with contempt the questions which are involved in those rights.[83]

One could say that Carwardine and others like him had not gone unnoticed, that indeed they had done what they hoped to do, reached the minds of those persons most prejudiced against the cause of labor.

Carwardine was appreciated by his congregation for the stand he took. On October 11, 1894, his congregation gave a reception for him, to which about 300 persons, representing all classes of Pullman society, came. Benjamin Ball gave an address of welcome on behalf of the congregation, praised the work of the pastor, and promised him support for his work in the future. The financial report of the church showed that it was clear of all debt, remarkable for the conditions in the town. The young people in the church, and a spokesman for town persons not in the Methodist Church, also expressed their appreciation for his work. Several of the other Pullman clergy were also present.[84]

On January 30, 1895, Carwardine delivered a lecture in New York in which he not only discussed the Pullman strike, but the very foundation of the industrial problem. He said the boycott or sympathetic strike was a wrong method of adjusting the difficulties of organized labor. For example, in the Pullman situation, labor flung itself with terrific force over against organized capital, and in the process the workers suffered greatly. However, speaking again as a good Populist and social gospel exponent, he said the main losers were the public. Society was too compact and interrelated in its interests to endure such a shock. The moment society's comforts, liberties, and cherished values were modified and interrupted, prejudice was engendered, class conflict set in, and sympathy was estranged from the cause of labor. Those elements of society which reacted in polarized fashion and condemned labor were wrong. At the same time, the thoughtful element of the wage-earning class would see at once, said Carwardine, that a general boycott which interfered with the publics' interests would always create the opportunity for the anarchistic and turbulent to introduce their bloody and insurrectionary tactics, and in the process, the cause of labor would suffer. In a time of excitement such as witnessed in Pullman, the public mind, alarmed and terrified, would be quick to condemn all strikers as anarchists. Therefore Carwardine did not agree with strikes or boycotts, but he made it clear that this did not mean he was against strikers. Strikers had to find more effective means to fight labor abuse.

The *Chicago Daily News* for September 17, 1895, carried an article concerning the upcoming Rock River Annual Conference of the Methodist Episcopal Church and the appointments that would be made. The article listed, as one of the major topics to be discussed, the "disposition of the Rev. W. H. Carwardine of Pullman." It was a miracle, the writer said, that last year Carwardine was kept in Pullman by the little money of impoverished strikers that could be contributed, and the liberal aid of a band of Methodist ministers. His Quarterly Conference the previous week had passed a resolution thanking Carwardine for staying in Pullman for three years. It now requested that the conference reward his "self-sacrifice" by an elevation to an "important charge." It is interesting that the *Pullman Journal,* according to the article, "willingly published this resolution in full." Could it be the *Journal's* editors looked forward to his removal?

The article mentioned some additional services provided by Carwardine which again illustrated his labor, social gospel concern. One of the major reasons for his remaining in Pullman was that he was director of the Homeseekers' Association. Many persons had wished to emigrate during the depressed conditions, and he had helped ;in the successful relocation of many Pullman families to different parts of the country. As a result, his parish dwindled from 300 to about 100 members, but he was looked upon as the pastor of all the oppressed at Pullman, and the church was still in good condition. The Rev. S. H. M. Coglan, one of Carwardine's warmest supporters and chairman of the committee that investigated the condition of those who wished to emigrate during the summer of 1894, said of Carwardine:

> Dr. Carwardine is one of our ablest and most brilliant orators. During his ministry he has built one church, two parsonages and raised several church debts, besides raising the exorbitant rent of $500 a year which Mr. Pullman asks for the present church, which, I understand, however, will be materially reduced as soon as Dr. Carwardine leaves. Several churches want him and his case will be dealt with early in the conference.[85]

It is interesting, if Coglan was right that the exorbitant rent charged the congregation, which had been cut by two thirds, would have been reduced as soon as Carwardine moved. Evidently the Pullman Company was anxious to see him go, to get rid of this thorn in its flesh. Undoubtedly Carwardine and his congregation were aware that it was necessary to reduce the financial burden on their small group of worshippers. There were, then, a number of motives behind the proposals for appointment of Carwardine to another church.

The *Toledo Union* for February 27, 1897, carried an interesting article entitled, "A Bit of Unwritten History." The point of the article, based on a lecture by Carwardine, was that the Pullman strike had certainly not been a complete failure. The struggle, Carwardine said, though it resulted in the defeat of the strikers, was not entirely lost. It had given rise to a great development in the study of sociological questions. Inquiry had been made, as a result of the strike, into the causes of industrial upheavals, and the further the inquiry progressed, the more favorable it would become for the workers. It had been proven that many of the grievances of the employees in Pullman were just beyond a doubt. Rents had been reduced, and that, said Carwardine, placed Mr. Pullman in an unenviable position, for during the strike he stated positively that it could not be done without a great loss to the company and therefore refused to arbitrate on the issue. The little two-room brick cottages, for which he charged $8 per month, and which were in plain view of travelers passing through the town, had been torn down. "They were too much of an object lesson, I suppose."[86]

However, said Carwardine, all was not well. Exorbitant gas and water rents were still charged, and the workers were still expected to live in Pullman homes. All the men working in Pullman shops now lived in Pullman, he said. "They are not told that they must do so, but if they do not they will not get any work." The hopeful sign was that public opinion was changing toward Pullman. The public opinion program that Carwardine had helped launch was bringing results.

He ended his lecture with a few words about Debs, who, he still insisted, was greatly misunderstood. He had known Debs well, and was in close deliberation with him. No man was more opposed to the strike than Debs, and time and time again he secured the floor of union meetings and advised against a strike. He described, "with almost prophetic vision," what the outcome would be, and what would happen to the workers' organization. "But the men were smarting under too many unjust wrongs to listen to reason, and they resolved to strike. And Eugene V. Debs, as president of the American Railway Union, carried out the wishes of the men." Carwardine said he believed, that had the advice of Debs been followed and the strike avoided, the conditions at Pullman would have been much improved. Had the public been fully acquainted with all the facts, the Pullman Company could not have withstood the demand for arbitration. However, the workers were living in deplorable conditions and were strained beyond the point of reason. "The boycott on Pullman cars, which resulted in the sympathetic strikes throughout the country was judged too harshly by many fair-minded people, who had heard little of the causes of the original trouble."[87]

The public must understand, insisted Carwardine, that men strike because of brutal treatment, because they don't like being made machines or cogs in wheels. Atrocious labor conditions produced the deterioration of the workers' homes, exhaustion, frustration, and thus upheaval.

Carwardine played an extremely significant and active role in the Pullman strike, as this chapter has endeavored to illustrate. He was motivated by, and contributed to, the labor, social gospel, and Populist movements. His activity was not to end with the Pullman strike. The manifestation of his value orientation on behalf of reform was deep and prolonged.

ENDNOTES

[1]William H. Carwardine, *The Pullman Strike* (Chicago: Charles H. Kerr and Co., 1984), p. 116,117.

[2]Leo Huberman, "The Have-Nots Versus the Haves." *Conflict or Consensus*, p. 113.

[3]Ibid., p. 114.

[4]Degler, p. 131

[5]Sel Yackley, "The Village that George Pullman Built," *Chicago Tribune Magazine*, (May 5, 1968), p. 85.

[6]Carwardine, *The Pullman Strike*, p. 34

[7]*Ibid.*, p. 35

[8]*Ibid.*, p. 36

[9]*Ibid.*, p. 37

[10]Almont Lindsey, *The Pullman Strike: the Story of a Unique Experiment and of a Great Labor Upheaval* (Chicago: University of Chicago Press, 1967), p. 124.

[11]"Preacher to Striker; Pullman Minister's Plain Words," *Chicago Herald*, May 21, 1894.

[12]*Ibid.*

[13]*Ibid.*

[14]Carwardine, *The Pullman Strike*, p. 38.

[15]Harvey Wish, "The Pullman Strike: a Study in Industrial Warfare," *Journal of the Illinois State Historical Society*, XXXII (September, 1939), p. 294.

[16]Carwardine, *The Pullman Strike*, p. 39

[17]Huberman, *Conflict or Consensus*, p. 116

[18]*United States Strike Commission Report on the Chicago Strike of June-July, 1894*, p. 180.

[19]Wish, p. 295.

[20]Carwardine, *The Pullman Strike*, p. 44.

[21]*Ibid.*, p. 45

[22]*Ibid.*, p. 46

[23]Lindsey, p. 320.

[24]*Ibid.*, p. 321

[25]*Northwestern Christian Advocate*, XLII (September 19, 1894).

[26]*Ibid.*

[27]*Ibid.*

[28]*Northwestern Christian Advocate*, XLII (May 2, 1894), p. 13.

[29]*Chicago Times*, May 20, 1894.

[30]*Carwardine*, The Pullman Strike, p. 14.

[31]"What the Ministers Said," *Chicago Daily News*, May 14, 1894.

[32]*Ibid.*

[33]*Ibid.*

[34]Carwardine, *The Pullman Strike*, p. 111

[35]*Chicago Times*, May 19, 1894.

[36]Carwardine, *The Pullman Strike*, p. 118

[37]*Chicago Herald*, May 21, 1894.

[38]*Ibid.*

[39]*Ibid.*

[40]*Ibid.*

[41]*Ibid.*

[42]*Ibid.*

[43]*Chicago Times*, May 22, 1894.

[44]*Ibid.*

[45]*Ibid.*

[46]*Ibid.*

[47]Carwardine, *The Pullman Strike*, introduction.

[48]Carwradine, *The Pullman Strike*, p. 20.

[49]*Ibid.*, p. 23.

[50]*Ibid.*, p. 25.

[51]*Ibid.*, p. 26.

[52]*Ibid.*, p. 31, 32.

[53]*Ibid.*, p. 49.

[54]*Ibid.*, p. 51-53.

[55]*Ibid.*, p. 54.

[56]*Ibid.*, p. 56.

[57]*Ibid.*, p. 58.

[58]*Ibid.*, p. 62, 63.

[59]*Ibid.*, p. 65.

[60]*Ibid.*, p. 67.

[61]*Ibid.*, p. 69.

[62]*Ibid.*, p. 72.

[63]*Ibid.*, p. 87.

[64]*Ibid.*, p. 92.

[65]*Ibid.*, p. 94.

[66]*Ibid.*, p. 98.

[67]*Ibid.*, p. 108.

[68]*Ibid.*, p. 122, 123.

[69]*Ibid.*, p. 123, 124.

[70]*Ibid.*, p. 124, 125

[71]*Ibid.*, p. 125.

[72]*Ibid.*, p. 126.

[73]*Ibid.*, p. 130.

[74]*United States Strike Commission Report on the Chicago Strike of June-July, 1894,* p. 448.

[75]*Ibid.*

[76]*Ibid.*, p. 449

[77]"Pastor vs. Pullman," *Chicago Tribune,* July 23, 1894.

[78]*Religious Philosophical Journal,* September, 1894.

[79]"Gift of Unpaid Rent," *Chicago Herald,* August 6, 1894.

[80]*Ellen County Mirror* (Ellen County, Texas), August 7, 1894.

[81]*Chicago Times,* September 11, 1894.

[82]*Ibid.*

[83]*Ibid.*

[84]*Chicago Record,* October 12, 1894, p. 8.

[85]*Chicago Daily News,* September 17, 1895.

[86]"A Bit of Unwritten History: the Rev. W. H. Carwardine Talks to the Pullman Strike," *Toledo Union,* February 27, 1897.

[87]*Ibid.*

CHAPTER V

CARWARDINE'S POST-STRIKE CONCERNS
AND ENDURING CONTRIBUTIONS

Carwardine traveled throughout the country delivering lectures on the industrial problem, and regularly wrote articles for newspapers. He approached the opening of the twentieth century with ambivalance. The new century, he said, would mark one of the most wonderful eras in the history of the world. However, just what would happen in the process was not certain. It was possible that the whole civilization in the United States might go to pieces, burst like a child's bubble by the inflation of its overwhelming materialistic pride and selfishness and thus lapse back again into a state of semi-barbarism. It was also possible that the American social condition might be so changed that if persons of the present generation could wake up some morning in the future after a long sleep, "like some Rip Van Winkle of the 20th century," they would think they had dropped down into a new world, in which some elements of the Christian millennium were evident. Either development was possible. Thus, while he manifested American optimism grounded on the values of providence, will, and nature, he was also skeptical as to whether or not Americans would be intelligent enough to let their destiny be realized. Radical changes had to take place in the relationship between labor and management, and between government and labor.

He warned that belief in providence ought not blind Americans to reality. There was no guarantee that America would not go the way of many other civilizations. There were, in fact, some remarkable similarities between the situation in the United States and that of other civilizations when they fell. For example, he said, when Egypt went down, two per cent of her population owned ninety-seven percent of her wealth. When Babylon went down, two per cent of her population owned all of her wealth. When Persia went down, one per cent of her population owned all her land. When Rome went down, 1,800 men owned all the known world. When the French revolution took place, there was aristocracy of wealth and birth on one side, and millions of half-fed, half-clad impoverished toilers on the other. Unless the United States mended her ways, and the "Christian conscience" of all classes was fully aroused to the real state of affairs, Carwardine feared that the United States would drift into the same channel.

On March 25, 1896, he delivered an address entitled "The Industrial Problem" to a gathering sponsored by the Federated Trades Council in Green Bay, Wisconsin. In the course of the address he denounced trusts, corporations, and monopolies, and he advocated the co-operative commonwealth, joint proprietorship, profit-sharing, and a condition of society based on the ethical principles of the "Sermon on the Mount" (Matthew 5-7, Luke 6:30-49 in the New Testament). Again he combined his concern for labor, the social gospel, and Populism. He told the audience that organization was the only hope for labor under the present conditions. Trades unions, he recognized, had built in dangers of their own. They had the tendency to be used, if not controlled, by "truckling leaders" for personal political ends, and to be arbitrary in their methods and demands. However, such unions should be heartily endorsed as long as their demands were "legitimate" and they recognized the authority of the law. If the wage earner did not organize to protect his interests, no one would do it for him.

Capital was still pooling its interests, and business was well organized. Business organizations bribed legislatures and influenced courts, so labor must apply pressure on behalf of its interests. There should be plenty of evidence, he said, for labor to realize the need for organization. Corporations ground labor into the dust through repeated wage reductions, and then on the slightest pretext had injunctions issued and the militia brought out to shoot labor down. Labor organizations had to protest and organize against modern centralization of wealth and power.

The United States had come under the control of an oligarchy, where a very small body of wealthy persons had come gradually to control the destiny of the country. "What then - an oligarchy! - in other words, a government in the hands of a few . . . the tendency to class legislation . . . Laws have been so shaped that wealth has been legislated out of the pockets of the masses into the coffers of the classes."[1] Speaking like a good Populist, Carwardine encouraged, in addition to labor organization, political action. "Ballots not bullets are the things that win in this country . . . A government of the people, for the people and by the people. Free schools - free speech - free press - free homes - free government."[2]

He carried his Populist and social gospel crusade into Muscatine, Iowa, where the *Muscatine Daily News-Tribune* covered his address. He continued his reform program by calling for tax reform. Corporate power, he said, was a menace to the welfare of a community when it sought to evade the just assessment valuation of its property. The corporation ought to be made to bear its full share of the state's burden. There ought to be a system of taxation by which the burdens of government fell fairly upon all people. The wealthier classes ought to bear the greater share of that burden in accordance with the principles of equity and justice. He recommended a properly regulated inheritance tax, and in spite of the Supreme Court's decision on the subject, recommended that an income tax be justly levied and enforced. He cited the case of the Pullman Company, which paid, annually, $200,000 less tax than it should.

He ended his discussion of tax reform with a phrase typical of the Populist camp. He believed that the hierarchy of values manifested in the United States' Declaration of Independence and Constitution had been reversed from their intended position. Property rights had taken precedence over human rights. "The rights of property are now warring on the rights of man."

Again, in the Populist tradition, he condemned "government by injunction" and the loss of liberty entailed. The cause of liberty had been grossly betrayed. Liberty had come to mean license to suppress others for one's benefit. Liberty had to be restored, he said, but must not be confused with lawlessness. Liberty was the largest exercise of individual freedom consonant with just laws, where there was absolute respect for the rights of men irrespective of social conditions.

Combining his social gospel orientation with that of Populism, Carwardine said that the "Golden Rule" (Matthew 7:12, Luke 6:31 in the New Testament) was the essence of true liberty. If there were one law for the rich man and another for the poor man, there was no liberty. True liberty was where the law incarnated the principle of doing unto others what you would have others do unto you.

He cited several examples where liberty had been lost. When a corporation, because it was wealthy and powerful, could control the vote of a senator or buy up a legislature, and thus defeat the will of the people, liberty was lost. When the president of a great university, like Chicago University, established by the profits of a "soulless, gigantic trust," whose business methods had been shown as a violation of the sacred rights and privileges of humanity, proceeded to oust a certain professor who dared to deal in "unvarnished terms with these evils" because it would interfere with the financial interests of the college, liberty was lost. When President Andrews of Brown University was forced to resign because his opinions on certain economic questions caused the university to be denied a certain donation from Mr. Rockefeller, according to many influential persons, liberty was lost. It seemed, said Carwardine, that the great capitalists were determined to capture free opinion through the nation's schools and press.

His combination of the social gospel and Populism was vividly displayed when he described Christ as the greatest political economist the world had ever known. Showing the basis of his "Christian socialism," he said the ideals of the Christian state were the ideals of the truly just society. The social revolution that was in process was leavened by Christianity and was the new coming of the kingdom of God. Sounding like a modern radical, he said: "Christ came to turn things upside down." Christian socialism was the only kind of socialism that could really help the workingman, socialism that was founded on the golden rule and the Sermon on the Mount.

Again Populism came to the fore when he warned the workers against depending on the major political parties for the cure of their ills. Too long, he said, had the workingmen of the country been subject to the beck and call of professional and selfish politicians, who, after they had gained their ends, flung the worker aside like an orange sucked of its juice and cast into the refuse pile. He warned against coalition politics, because political parties had played fast and loose with labor's interests. Instead of feeling they must align themselves with a major political party, they ought to display political independence in the organization of and support of parties which genuinely represented the ideals advocated by the workingmen. Carwardine believed that the Populist-oriented programs were most beneficial to labor's needs. Independence, he said, was not fidelity to the way things had always been done. Because a thing had been done for a long time was no evidence that it must always be done. The grandest results and most beneficient achievements in the history of the race were won by independence and the independent man. He cited, as examples, such persons as Columbus, John Howard, George Washington, Patrick Henry, Daniel Webster, Wendell Phillips, and Abraham Lincoln. Again he made it clear, that "ballots not bullets" were the things that won battles in the United States.

He also spoke to the matter of woman and child labor from several angles. He felt that economic selfishness and corporate greed were the main sources of women and child labor, because it was cheaper labor than that of men. The results were bad for many reasons. Factory life sapped the physical and moral being of women and children, and was detrimental to family life. It increased the mortality rate of women and children. It made women and children unfit for family life because it weakened home interests and encouraged the neglect of home duties. A major problem caused by woman and child labor was that it destroyed the family role of the male wage earner. Men had difficulty finding work because employers would hire the cheaper woman and child labor, and the consequential loss of the chief "bread winner" role for many men had serious psychological results. Carwardine said it was the combination of all the problems he discussed and the refusal of government intervention on behalf of the worker that crushed the heart of the American wage earner and drove him to the adoption of the "extreme socialistic" views.

On September 17, 1896, Carwardine addressed a large crowd at Kalamazoo, Michigan, on its annual celebration of National Labor Day. He spoke of the great class conflict in America, where selfishness dominated, where patriot was turned against patriot calling each other anarchist and socialist. In spite of the continuing conflict, there was progress, and the Pullman event, he believed, had done more than anything else in modern history to awaken a patriotic consideration of the questions relating to industrial conditions. He again stated his belief in arbitration, but said great corporations like the Pullman Company had strongly arrayed themselves against arbitration on the ground that no man should interfere with another in the so called right to run his business to suit himself. Though some progress had been made, laissez faire capitalism and the modified American values accompanying it still predominated.

Carwardine believed that laissez faire capitalism, which placed the right of the individual above the best interests of society as a whole, could not last much longer. Again his argument was Populist-oriented, and sounded much like modern rationales for closer co-operation. He believed that society was so complete, business interests were so closely allied, and the welfare of all classes were becoming so "fearfully intermingled" in the great cities especially, that no employer of labor and no corporation had the right nor would dare to run his business to suit himself and withhold from a vast army of employees the right of arbitration, the privilege to submit their difficulties to an impartial board legally organized for such purposes by the state.

Carwardine was somewhat influenced by the nativism of the times, but he was also illustrative of the fact that persons associated with Populism have been too generally categorized as extreme nativists. For example, he spoke of the problems created by the importation of cheap foreign labor. The tremendous influx of foreign elements brought old-world ideas and notions that produced political, social and industrial havoc, said Carwardine. In thinking this way he was representative of his age, and not just of Populists. Built into the American value of "nature" was the superiority of the American because he was free of "decadent Europe." Nativism was not unique to Populists, and when Carwardine spoke of the "introduction into American life of all those anti-American notions that are brought here by the rabble - the off-scouring of Europe," he was manifesting a value held by most Americans. It is important to note that Carwardine went on from there to say that all Americans were foreigners more or less. He said:

There is very little of what may be termed pure American stock left. And yet there is an immense amount of Americanism in this land of ours . . . . Americanism is a factor in the world today. It has a decided meaning, and one of which we ought to be proud. Into this connection has mingled the blood of many nationalities.. . . To the better element among our foreign born citizens America owes much of her greatness today. England, Ireland, Scotland and Wales, Germany, France, Sweden, Norway and Holland have thrown some of their best blood into American life to make this nation what it is today. It is these men who have plowed our soil, filled our granaries . . . but the emigration that brings us a horde of pauper laborers to compete with native labor is detrimental, and productive of harm between employer and employee. All honor to the man who comes here to make his home among us, and become a citizen of this country and to become a part of us. I refer to those who only come here to get what they can out of us. Intelligent American labor is at the mercy of this partly criminal, partly respectable hoard of pauper labor *imported by great corporations and railroads.* This introduction of cheap pauper labor introduces other elements of serious consideration into this industrial problem.[3] (italics mine)

The point is, what Carwardine was chiefly concerned about was not the national origin of peoples, but the fact that many came to the United States only on the invitation of corporations who hoped to exploit them and as a result to exploit American laborers who would not work for the same low wages and poor conditions. It was the "exploitive presence" of cheap labor that he felt was un-American. If foreign stock became citizens and part of the normal labor force, then they were seen to have contributed to labor and thus to the greatness of America. However, when they competed with the American labor force, they were seen to have been "un-American." It was the "usage" of such cheap labor by corporations that was seen to have been remnants of "old world serfdom."

Carwardine again reminded his listeners that the day of true liberty, when the rights of all people, irrespective of sex, condition and color, and the right of every man to express his opinion on vital issues in "temperate" language in public without fear of ostracism, was far from realization. However, in the movement toward this day of liberty, of which he saw himself a part, the workers should remember, that "the best friend of humanity and the laborer is . . . Christ." Again one sees here the combination of labor, social gospel, and Populist influences. Carwardine lashed out at professors of religion, clergymen, and laymen who through their hypocrisy, unholy lives and false pretenses, sham tendencies and dead formalism, caused the masses to feel that Christianity was a delusion and only for the wealthier classes.

Again he emphasized his belief in the principles of co-operation, co-operative manufacturing plants, and co-operative stores. He stressed that the government should take control of the railroad and telegraph systems of the country, and that city municipalities should direct and control city railroads and gas companies. Carwardine was moving further along Populist lines in his program of "Christian socialism."

Throughout the year of 1897 Carwardine continued to give lectures and write newspaper articles for the cause of labor. The content of his speeches was similar to those already discussed. For example, one of the newspaper headings over a summary of his speech read: "Says Future is Dark - Carwardine the Pullman Divine Talks on Labor - He Says the Only Safety of the Laborer is in Organization - Unequal and Unjust Distribution of Wealth - Was a Rattling Speech." Again he expounded upon a Populist theme, that the hierarchy of American values had been reversed, and property rights had superseded human rights. The individual, he said, meant nothing in the laissez faire philosophy.

At a speech given in Oshkosh, Wisconsin, on September 11, 1897, he again attacked those persons who would see labor dissent and reform advocates as subversive. He insisted that it was the patriotic duty of every citizen to study the condition of the country and point out its strong and weak points, for only then could the nation progress. Nations, like individuals, had their sins, and sins were enemies. A nation's sins were like diseases which threatened its very life. The inequalities of life in America, as indicated in the social fabric, were cancers that were consuming its vital energies. When industry, and the nation's populace, suppressed labor, it was sapping the life blood of the whole society.[4]

Carwardine delivered an address in Sioux City, Iowa, on March 31, 1898, in which he made careful distinctions between his "Christian socialism" and other socialistic tendencies of the day. He said he was afraid of the socialism founded upon the teachings of Karl Marx which appealed to many workmen. Marx's socialism was a materialistic socialism, and he would rather not live at all than live in a society of "inane dead levelism." "Such a condition may be pleasant to dream about - a Utopia for the enthusiast, but such a condition will never be realized in this hard work-a-day world with human nature full of aspiration and activity."[5] Again he affirmed his "Americanism" and his basic acceptance of free enterprise. He was afraid that the loss of free enterprise would cause a loss of individual aspiration. He tended to accept the "Horatio Alger" notion to the extent that if most any person were given a real opportunity, he could succeed, but laissez faire capitalism did not give equal opportunity. Carwardine accepted many of the basic values of the day, but wanted to strip them of their laissez faire distortion. He also wanted more government regulation.

Rather than Marxian socialism, he recommended the "socialism of the Sermon on the Mount." Christian socialism was what American society needed, and he saw the transition toward this goal as a true manifestation of the traditional values of providence, nature, and will. America was unique by providence, and it was to be the battleground for the settlement of the social inequalities of mankind on the basis of Christian socialism. Americans were an intelligent people, had read history, and thus knew the failures of the past. The extremes of wealth and poverty were agitating the minds of many people, and thus the time was ripe, and indeed it was happening; people were seeing that when Christ gave the Sermon on the Mount and his other social teachings, he proved himself to have been not only a teacher of morals but a teacher of economics. Carwardine affirmed that Christ was the greatest political economist the world had ever seen.

The most disastrous attitude a person could have was that society had to continue unchanged. Defense of the status quo was the death of America's promised greatness, for it ended progress. Christ came to turn things upside down, and that was just what American society needed. The purpose of Christian socialism, in a few words, was to unite "the truth of God's human fatherhood, and man's divine sonship, with the brotherhood of need and service."[6]

Carwardine ended his speech with a plea that the workmen of America would, in their own organizations, elect true leaders and put away petty jealousies and quarrels. He encouraged them to move toward Populist-oriented reform party programs, to work for legislation which would change some of the economic and industrial inequalities that existed. He also had another word to say about Debs. Debs, he insisted, was a great man. "I believe him to be as honest as the multiplication table, and to have at heart no other purpose than to benefit those in whose behalf he was enlisted." However, Debs' problem was that he was too idealistic in what he hoped to accomplish and when:

> He is so much in advance of what can be the popular judgment, so far as methods are concerned, that he is unable to accomplish all that he has hoped. His sympathies are quick and profound, but he allows them to make him impracticable, in my judgment, and they lead him into declarations and acts which I fear do not help the cause. What is needed at this time is good hard practical sense instead of inflammable agitation. I admire Debs for what he wants to do, but question some of the ways by which he wants to do it.[7]

Of course, it is common to have agreement between reformers as to the ends, but differences of opinion as to the means to accomplish the ends. After the Pullman strike and the Supreme Court's upholding of Debs' conviction for contempt, Debs tended to become more angry with the status quo, less optimistic as to the rate of change, and thus more radical in his denunciations and suggestions for change. Carwardine understood why Debs took this course of action, but did not agree with it and believed it would do more harm than good for the labor cause.

He also had some comments for another "Christian socialist," the Rev. F. L. Herron of Grinnel, Iowa. Herron had achieved renown for his agitation in the name of Christian socialism, but Carwardine found him to be somewhat of a dreamer also. Dreams were fine, in terms of millennial ends, but in this life, one must set practical, reachable goals, he insisted. Herron, he said, was impractical:

He is another man who is a dreamer, but a lovable personage. He wants to accomplish a tremendous good in the world, but he seeks to establish at this time a condition which will be possible only when the millennium shall have arrived. We have to deal with things as they are, and not as we would wish them to be. Mr. Herron's 'Christian commonwealth' is a beautiful conception, but we of today must do the work which is close at hand, and not attempt to establish now those conditions which, if possible at all, can come only to future generations and centuries.[8]

The year 1899 was also filled with speech-making and article-writing. On April 30 Carwardine addressed a gathering called by the Central Trades Council in Marion, Indiana. To illustrate that his cause was truly American, the speaker's desk was draped with the American flag. He again encouraged organization and political action, condemned woman and child employment practices, and attacked capital's attempt to control free opinion and criticism of its actions through the pulpit, press, and universities. He lashed out at government by injunction and proposed his reform programs.

The newspaper heading above a description of another speech given in Indiana read: "Elicited Applause - Rev. Carwardine Spoke - For the Cause of Labor - Present Tendency is Toward Oligarchy." The content of the address was similar to his others, but, reflecting the fear of anarchistic uprisings whenever dissent was expressed, he emphasized particularly that he advocated change by evolution and not revolution. "The discontent with the present system is growing but the change for better will come by evolution, not revolution." However, he left no doubt that change would come, and that it would be in the direction of increased government control. The trusts and monopolies had brought this upon themselves, indeed had hastened the movement, because "financial combination has overreached itself, and will result in reaction. The trust is a diagonal short-cut to public control of facilities." Of course, consistent with his program of Christian socialism, he stated that the remedy of social disorders would come through the establishment of socialism based on the command, "thou shalt love thy neighbor as thyself."

On August 9, 1899, according to the *Bulletin* of Muncie, Indiana, he addressed the largest crowd that had ever greeted a labor orator in the history of organized labor in Muncie. A writer for the *Trades Journal* of Muncie said Carwardine was a master of his art, that he held the audience entranced by the power of his words for nearly two hours, and that his arguments were the most logical ever produced by the mind of man. He was invited to return for another address on labor problems later in the year.

From 1900 until his death, Carwardine continued his writing and lecturing. However, in 1904, he launched into a new field, and ran as a candidate for state representative of Illinois. Often he had spoken of active political involvement, and now he tried to increase his involvement from that of writing and speaking to office holding. This was fitting for one with such a Populist, social gospel orientation, an orientation that directed him into a unique political stand. He was nominated by the Prohibition Party as its candidate for the legislature in the 27th district. It will be remembered, however, that the Prohibition Party was one of those involved in the Populist coalition. Carwardine was able to direct his Christian socialism and Populism into a political party that was supported by the church, labor, and other Populist-oriented groups.

His nomination by the Prohibition Party was made without his knowledge, and his first inclination was to refuse the nomination. However, many of his friends insisted that he accept it, which finally he did. The *Chicago Fireman's Journal* for September 22, 1904, said, upon his acceptance: "There exists no doubt but that his personal following will rally to his support and elect him to the position for which he is nominated." The *Journal* pointed out that this was not the first time he had been approached to run for a political office, and wrote:

> At the time of the strike, the voters of the Pullman district urged him to allow his name to be presented before a convention of the independents as their candidate. This move he emphatically vetoed. Had he, however, allowed his admirers to go ahead, it is a safe assertion that his election would have been practically unanimous, as the working men were worked up to a pitch such as had never before occurred and were standing by each other and their champions so loyally and faithfully that it required the expenditure of millions of corporate wealth to purchase the power to subdue them.[9]

A word should be said about the Prohibition Party. The Women's Christian Temperance Union, founded in 1874 and soon thereafter led by Frances E. Willard, took the lead in the anti-liquor movement. Other groups joined in the crusade, and the National Prohibition Party which had been founded in 1869 thus received added support and ran a presidential candidate regularly. The Anti-Saloon League of America, founded in 1895, added further support. However, the progress of the Prohibition Party was slight, as only Kansas and North Dakota joined Maine, New Hampshire, and Vermont in statewide prohibition between 1860 and 1900. It must be remembered, however, that there were many reform movements taking place in the late 1800's, and advocates of reform such as Carwardine and Willard crossed the lines of many different movements. Many persons concerned with prohibition were also concerned with labor conditions, women's rights, discrimination, and other causes. Carwardine was one of these diversified reformers. While he was concerned with prohibition, he was also concerned about many other problems, so it was easy for him to identify with a particular party but with a much broader program in mind. That is, he was an excellent representative of the type of reformers who met to draw up the Populist platform at Omaha, Nebraska, in July of 1892. The Populists represented a coalition of many reform groups, among them being the National Alliance, the Northern Alliance, the Knights of Labor, the Prohibitionists, and the Greenbackers. Carwardine as an individual represented a diversification of concerns.

Carwardine's platform was an excellent manifestation of his labor, social gospel, Populist orientation. A leaflet which described his platform read:

> Mr. Carwardine will stand for the principle of prohibition. He will favor any bill which will give the people of any locality a chance to do away with the saloon evil. He will stand for all just and equitable laws in the interest of labor. He will favor legislation against those trusts that have for their goal a monopoly of the necessaries of life. He favors any good law that will put an end to the loan-shark evil. He will stand by the rights of the people in all matters of strict railway legislation, public ownership, and civil service. He favors the initiative and the referendum. He will stand for the new charter amendment.[10]

All of these planks were strongly influenced by Populist/Progressive and social gospel thought.

The leaflet went on to list the endorsements of Carwardine, illustrating that only he was the "people's" candidate. Of the four candidates, he was the one endorsed by the Legislative Voters' League in the 27th Legislative District. He also had official endorsements from many labor organizations, such as city trade and labor councils of the American

Federation of Labor from over sixty cities throughout the United States. He was endorsed by President Samuel Gompers of the American Federation of Labor and a host of others "who admire and recognize his earnest effort in the interest of the wage earner." The leaflet listed the other three candidates, two Democrats and one Republican, and illustrated how their platforms conflicted with Carwardine's and thus with the best interests of the people. He was described as the "people's" candidate, which of course was the image projected by the "People's Party" (Populists).[11]

The front page of the leaflet was interesting. It had a picture of Carwardine with a marked voting box beside it, accompanied by the words: "Vote for W. H. Carwardine, 'The Friend of Labor.'" The leaflet encouraged voters to break out of the major party habit with the words: "Be a good enough American Citizen to vote for a good man on an opposite ticket where there is a bad man on your own ticket." Such a view was consistent with Carwardine's emphasis upon independent balloting and suspicion of the major parties that would "use labor" to get votes and then betray them with legislation favorable to corporation interests.

Carwardine enjoyed and saved a defaced leaflet that had been placed in one of the local bars. His nose had been painted red, his face whiskered, and a bum's hat placed on his head. Obviously the point was to illustrate the irony of a leaflet hanging in a bar asking the patrons to vote for a Prohibition candidate. Beneath the words, "Vote for W. H. Carwardine, 'The Friend of Labor,'" were written the words, "why certainly, who the hell wouldn't." Carwardine was running on the Prohibition ticket, but the workers frequenting the bar knew that his reform programs far exceeded prohibition and that he was indeed the friend of labor.

The *Chicago Fireman's Journal* was emphatic in its endorsement of Carwardine and encouraged its readers to vote for him. He was a fearless friend of the firemen who had done much for the twelve-hour day, it stated.

He was a fearless defender of the worker in general; "a God-fearing man, he possesses the moral courage to express his views on all subjects regardless of their popularity. The years of his life have been devoted unselfishly for the betterment of his fellowmen. His standing among all classes of men proves in no uncertain manner that his labors in behalf of humanity have not been in vain." The *Journal* went on to say why firemen and policemen, in addition to industrial workers, supported Carwardine:

His record proves that at all times, in all places, he had the welfare, the betterment, the happiness of the common people at heart. His ringing denunciation of the unscrupulous acts of corporate power have had the effect of correcting abuses which had existed for years. His labors on behalf of the firemen of this city are still fresh in the minds of the people. His forceful articles in the *Chicago Examiner*, which were served to the readers of that great journal every morning for breakfast, awakened the people of Chicago to a realization that they were permitting a system to exist which would disgrace the hardest task-master of ante-bellum days. The articles in the *Examiner* and *American* informed the people of Chicago that the firemen were actually working twenty-one hours in every twenty-four. To thousands this was news they had never heard before. It is an actual fact that thousands of people in this city were under the impression that the fire department was worked by two shifts of men, which alternated in working nights and day. Mr. Carwardine's articles educated them to a point where the average citizen has a fairly accurate idea of how the fire department is run, at least as regards the hours of labor.[12]

The article went on to remind its readers that Carwardine had awakened people's lethargy through his articles and addresses, and it was lethargy on the part of the public which had allowed abuses to grow into customs which were very difficult to eradicate.

Certain corruptions were pointed out that were going to hurt Carwardine's chances of being elected. The 27th district was abnormally shaped, due to intentional gerrymandering, so as to aid the incumbent party candidate and hurt the chances of others. Thus the article encouraged every workman, policeman, and fireman to get out and vote since the cards were stacked against them anyway. "In some cases the fortunes of politics has thrown their friends into spots where the united efforts of the entire number cannot be concentrated. Such is the condition in the case of Mr. Carwardine. He is nominated in the 27th Senatorial District. This district is a sort of shoestring affair. . . ."[13] The district had been gerrymandered in order to prevent a concentration of voters to the type favorable to Carwardine.

A campaign letter circulated by A. W. Fairbanks, Carwardine's campaign manager, is of great importance in illustrating the support Carwardine had stirred and the impact of his reform programs. The letter was circulated by the Campaign Headquarters, Twenty-Seventh Senatorial District, A. W. Fairbank, Campaign Manager, and was dated from Chicago, November 1, 1904. It was circulated just prior to election day, and is of enough importance to quote in its entirety:

> Dear Sir: We take pleasure in calling your attention to the candidacy of W. H. Carwardine, of the Eighteenth Ward, for election to the Illinois legislature in the Twenty-Seventh Senatorial District. He is a friend of the laboring man. His national reputation which he obtained in the great Pullman strike of 1894, has easily made him the peer of any man in

Chicago in his manner of presenting the cause of the wage earner. He is one of the best posted men in the city on questions of this character and his years of opportunity and experience have added to his ability. The wage earner can trust him to guard well his interests. He will be against any gang or gavel rule, and will see that the money of the tax-payer is not wasted. His advocacy last winter of the double twelve hour shift for the firemen of Chicago has won him a host of friends on the fire and police department of Chicago.

Enclosed you will find a folder giving his history, platform, endorsements and the records of his opponents. Since his candidacy was first announced, citizens of all parties have signified their intention of supporting him.

The coming legislative session is to be one of the most important in the history of the state. We appeal to you without reference to party. Read the statement of the Legislative Voters' League as to the character of his opponents. Vote your party preference in national affairs, but scratch for your legislature. It means three votes for Mr. Carwardine. If you are favorable, vote for him, work for him, and if possible sign and mail us the enclosed enrollment card.[14]

Carwardine lost the election. Many persons blamed the incumbent "machine's" gerrymandering and unethical campaigning, and said it was another example of big business conspiring against labor by helping to elect a puppet for its own usage. In spite of the loss, Carwardine kept his own personal campaign going - through speaking and writing on behalf of labor and other causes. The *Chicago Register-Gazette* for October 2, 1920, made a biting satire on Carwardine which at the same time illustrated his reform activity in diverse areas. In an editorial, reference was made to the

Chicago preacher-news writer, who was waging his "war against sin." Carwardine was, at this time, not only a pastor but religious editor for the *Chicago Herald and Examiner.* He had served as religious editor since 1905, and in the process had irritated many persons who felt he should "mind his own business" and not try to solve the world's economic, political, and social problems. Carwardine said that working on the solution of such problems was the business of Christian pastors, and certainly his Christian socialism was built on that belief. The *Register-Gazette* editorial referred to one of Carwardine's social statements and said: "So here you are, folks. Permit us to introduce the typewriting pastor who wages his battle against Satan from his pulpit in Chicago on Sundays and the rest of the week days through the columns of a Chicago morning newspaper."[15] Carwardine saw himself as doing just that, waging a battle through pulpit and press against sin, manifested in the social, political, and economic life of the time.

The main focus of our discussion has been Carwardine's reform activities as they affected the labor scene. However, as stated earlier, his concerns crossed many lines. The columns he wrote for the *Herald and Examiner* illustrated the breadth of his concern. For example, in 1923 he referred to the tragic death of Wallace Reid who had won fame through his rendition of "Peter Ibbetson" on the screen, and through many other fine works. Carwardine referred to Reid's use of dope, and the headline to his column read: "Reid's End; Our Duty - Will Wally's Destruction Arouse Us to Stamp Out Demon Dope, or are We Helpless?" No matter what issue Carwardine was writing about, he managed to bring in his reform concern. His social gospel, Populist orientation pervaded all that he did. In reference to Reid and the dope issue, he again appealed for government action:

> What about a nation that encourages the sale of opium? What about a government that will thrust it upon a defenseless people that they may have revenues to spend at home? What

about officials who are derelict in their duty to the community in the fight against this demon of dope? What of the low scoundrels who peddle it. . . . Will the death of Wallace Reid help in the fight on dope? Will it aid in arousing the conscience of the nation to greater activity in the passage of laws so stringent that the evil will be eradicated?[16]

Another of Carwardine's columns dealt with bad housing conditions in New York City, Chicago, and other urban centers. Such conditions, he said, encouraged immorality and disease. In this column he expressed another theory common for reformers of the age - environmentalism. George Pullman was an environmentalist in asserting that his company town could produce the kind of workman with the "proper values" that would destroy the basis for labor unrest. It is interesting that critics of Pullman's system and other industrial problems used the same environmental argument. Environment did affect human character, for good and for bad. Some industrial problems were the results of planned environment, such as that of Pullman, with its built-in paternalism. Other industrial problems were the result not of a planned but of a poor environment that accompanied an unregulated industrial system. Just as the environment produced problems, the solution to problems lay in creating a new environment. The government was responsible for creating that new environment. "Environment is not everything, but it is an essential element in the development of character," Carwardine often insisted.

He spoke of the environmental problem in many different contexts. One article entitled, "When the Parents Fail," concerned the situation created in the home and the impact it had on children. He referred to a plea from a mother in Oak Park, Illinois, one of the more "refined, cultured" communities in the Chicago area. The mother asked for the protection of the community's "virtuous young boys from the unrestrained high school girls," puppy love adventures, petting parties, and "other unconventionalities indulged in by the lads and lassies." Carwardine said that this was simply another indication of the problem confronting all of society. Vice was vice, he said, whether in beautiful homes or in ordinary hovels. "Environment, marvelous as is its influence, is still lacking. Education and culture and refining influences, worthwhile as they are, cannot take the place of the real mother and father and the right kind of home."[17]

Carwardine had said earlier that, due to his treatment during the Pullman strike and the ensuing court action, and to the seemingly impossible hold corporations had on the government, Eugene Debs had become much more radical. Though he understood why Debs did what he did, he disagreed with him. During the First World War, he said, Debs had denounced the war and uttered some "ugly things about governments in general." He was an extremist and an idealist, but was also theoretical and prophetic in his visions touching the matters of industrial, social, and economic conditions. He was sincere, honest, and had a heart and soul as clean as a child's, but temperamentally he was explosive and "he ran diametrically counter to sober judgment in a trying period of the nation's history." Debs saw himself, and Carwardine agreed, as patriotic and ready to die for his ideas just as did John the Baptist, Savonarola, and John Brown. However, in the passionate period of the war, his words and actions were taken as dangerous and subversive, and he was placed in the Atlanta penitentiary.

Carwardine tried to make his own point of view clear. He wanted to see a movement to have Debs released from the penitentiary, because he had committed no crime. "During the excitement of the war thousands of men said things far more unpatriotic than Debs, and were not jailed." Carwardine believed that Debs was put in prison because of his earlier and continuous fight for the labor cause in addition to his unpopular stand on the war. It was damnable that a man was imprisoned because he honestly held an unpopular stand on the war. It was ridiculous to consider him a threat or an aid to the enemy. "Freedom of speech, freedom of the press and a right to explore one's visionary notions has nothing to fear from the rank and file of the American people, who laugh at Bolshevism and the vagaries of radicalism." Carwardine said he did not agree with much of what Debs said anymore, but he knew him to be an honest man who expressed what, in his opinion, would make for a better America.

Perhaps, Carwardine said, he himself had become more conservative with the passing of years and that was why he disagreed with Debs. However, he defended Debs' right to say what he wished to say:

> I have no sympathy with much that Debs believes. It was dangerous to utter such sentiments at a time when Europe was on fire and America threatened. But I knew Eugene Debs during the dark days of the Pullman strike, in 1894. I made many speeches with him, on the same platform. I believed in the man, but not in all he said. I have lived long enough to realize some of us who were called anarchists in those days as touching things industrial and social reform are the conservatives of today.[18]

Carwardine never lost his prohibition interests. In a column for the *Chicago Herald and Examiner* in 1927, he gave his prohibition views as they related to President Coolidge. Carwardine, it will be remembered, ran on the Prohibitionist Party ticket in 1904. Now that the Eighteenth Amendment had been passed, he was quite happy, but thought the law was not being enforced effectively. He blamed the president for this laxity, and stated his agreement with an editorial appearing in *Christian Century* which lashed out at President Coolidge. President Coolidge had disappointed many persons, he said. There was no national prohibition in any true sense, because Coolidge did not greatly care whether the nation had it or not. The president was "studiously indifferent," and had not given proper leadership. Therefore Carwardine agreed with the article in the *Christian Century* and advocated a different candidate for the presidency in 1928 who would "win the victory for law enforcement."

While Carwardine served a church in LaSalle, Illinois, in the year 1925, he wrote critically of American drinking problems. He praised the Eighteenth Amendment and called upon his listeners to support the Constitution of which the Eighteenth Amendment was a part. He said, in answer to someone's questions as to the chances of repeal, that he didn't think the amendment would ever be repealed; definitely not! Laws had to be obeyed.

Carwardine's concern for reform, extending from his labor, social gospel and Populist orientation, was a continual concern, as this chapter has illustrated. Not only that, he left many enduring contributions. He left his mark upon American society.

-CARWARDINE'S ENDURING CONTRIBUTIONS-

William H. Carwardine was born on February 22, 1858, in Brooklyn, New York, the son of William James and Catherine Elliott Carwardine. His parents died when he was very young, so he was much on his own. He attended public schools in New York and then went on to attend private schools in Ramsgate and Gloucester, England. He was a student at Colgate University in Hamilton, New York and Peter Cooper Institute in New York City. On September 27, 1880, he married Elizabeth Williams of Brooklyn, New York, and they gave birth to two sons, Chester and Arthur.

Carwardine was ordained a minister of the Methodist Episcopal Church in 1882 and became a member of the South Kansas Annual Conference of the Methodist Episcopal Church. He served pastorates in

Kansas from 1882 to 1887. He then traveled to Illinois for his theological training, and graduated from Garrett Biblical Institute, in Evanston, in 1889. He was transferred to the Rock River Annual Conference of the Methodist Episcopal Church in Illinois, and served pastorates in Steward and Poplar Grove for one year each; LaSalle for four years; and several churches in Chicago, including Pullman, Ada Street, Adams Street, Forty-Seventh Street, Gross Park, Humboldt Park, South Chicago, Windsor Park, and Hermosa Methodist Church.

During the Pullman strike, he attacked the Pullman Company and defended the striking workers. His book, *The Pullman Strike*, was published in 1894. He was a key witness in the United States Strike Committee's investigation and his testimony and part of his book were incorporated into the commission's report, which was given to Congress in November of 1894. During and after the Pullman strike he became widely known in the United States and abroad in matters of industrial economics. He lectured on this subject in 64 cities under the auspices of trade and labor organizations, Chautauquas, and clubs. Throughout the Chicago area he spoke to civic, labor, church and other groups and was a frequent guest preacher.

He became the religious editor of the *Chicago Herald and Examiner*, one of the first of such positions, and contributed daily signed articles from 1905 on, extending his ministry far beyond that of a normal pastor. He seemed to have the ability to put his finger on the pulse of the world and gave meaningful interpretations. He was a leader in bringing the church to a frontal position in social consciousness.

There were many incidents early in his life which indicated the presence of courage and persistence that were to make themselves manifestly evident in later years. For example, when he was attending Peter Cooper Institute (Cooper Union for the Advancement of Science and Art) in New York City, he failed an important examination. Some interesting correspondence then took place between him and the administration of the school. He wrote to Mr. Peter Cooper, president of the school, and said he felt it was his duty to express his sorrow for such a failure. It was a wretched blow to him, and "mortification, disgust, and discouragement have been the natural result." He said he hoped that in the future, he might bring honor and not disgrace to the institute. This, of course, he was to do.

A response to his letter came from Mr. J. C. Zachus. He said that Mr. Cooper wanted to express his sympathy with Carwardine's sense of failure that he seemed to feel so deeply. It was a good sign that his reaction was not one of indifference. He assured him that he had not failed for the same reason that many students had done, lack of effort and desire. He had failed because he had not put his manuscript into Zachus' hands before taking the examining stand. If he had given his instructor the manuscript, he would have saved himself the embarrassment. Mr. Zachus ended by asking Carwardine to keep this maxim in mind: "True greatness consists, not in never falling, but in always rising after a fall."[19]

Carwardine never did forget that maxim. Certainly the labor cause, and he himself, in the midst of the strike, public reaction, and political activity, had many falls. He always rose after the fall. In fact, he never felt he had fallen, but had only a few temporary setbacks.

Evidence of Carwardine's intellectual potential that was to be manifestly evident in years to come could be seen in a letter he received from Mr. J. Hampden Dougherty on May 22, 1879, suggesting his achievements at Cooper Institute far outweighed his failures. Mr. Dougherty, an attorney and counsellor at law in New York, wrote to Carwardine and congratulated him for his intellectual achievement and his selection as the representative of the institute to travel to the capital. Dougherty said he was sure that Carwardine in the future would be a real success.[20] Certainly Dougherty did not know how prophetic he was. He later served as a reference for Carwardine when he planned to enter the ministry, and wrote many letters on his behalf testifying to his superior character.

Just prior to his moving into the Chicago area, Carwardine had served a church in Greeley, Kansas. Upon his departure from Greeley to attend Garrett Biblical Institute, the Greeley congregation expressed its appreciation for his leadership and indicated that it knew he would emerge as a leader within the church. The local newspaper, the *Greeley News*, printed, on September 4, 1886, this resolution:

> Resolutions of Respect, Greeley, Anderson Co., Kansas, September 4, 1886. Whereas, the Rev. W. H. Carwardine has served us as pastor and preacher of this charge for the past eighteen months, acceptably, and is now about to leave us to pursue a course of studies at the Evanston Biblical Institute [Garrett Biblical Institute was in Evanston, Illinois] to better fit himself for his life's work; therefore, resolved, that we, the officials and other members of the Methodist Episcopal Church, very reluctantly consent to his leaving this charge, and that we bid him God-speed in his new undertaking and hope he may be successful in the same. That we cordially recommend him to the brethren of the Methodist Episcopal Church wherever he may be called to serve, and we feel assured that he will faithfully and honestly perform all the duties as preacher and pastor.[21]

Carwardine died on Sunday, August 25, 1929, and was buried in Memorial Park Cemetery, Evanston, Illinois. The material presented in this book speaks to the lasting contributions he made to American society. He of course did not single-handedly change American society, and indeed he did not see many of the changes that he hoped to see, but which were eventually to materialize. However, he was a member of a small but very dedicated and persistent group of reformers who together were to have a tremendous impact upon American society. The labor movement, social gospel, Christian socialism, and Populism were to alter greatly the American scene, and Carwardine was a part of them. He was inspired by these movements, and he contributed to them. He was a part of that group of reformers who created and manifested a transition of values in the late 1800's and early 1900's. He saw himself as a good loyal American who accepted traditional values basic to America's uniqueness and greatness. However, he believed that the society of his day had distorted those values to serve big business' vested interests. One might say that Carwardine and his kind were attempting to do what some reformers today are attempting to do, not destroy American society or American capitalism, but put capitalism behind the Constitution where it was meant to be, and not ahead of the Constitution where in practice it has often been. Carwardine rebelled against the reversal in the hierarchy of American values that characterized laissez faire capitalism in the late 19th and 20th centuries. He abhorred the fact that property rights had superseded human rights and demanded that the situation be corrected. He knew there were certain ways in which reform could be implemented. For his basic orientation, rationale, and methodology he turned to the social gospel and Populism, and developed what he called Christian socialism. The government had to take a more active role in regulation and move toward more public co-operation, ownership, and direct political involvement. The relationship between labor and management, government and the governed, and all human concerns, had to be based on the principle of the golden rule and the ethics of the Sermon on the Mount.

There is no doubt that the values manifested in Carwardine and the movements with which he was so closely related - labor, the social gospel, and Populism - had a tremendous impact on American society. A transition in values occurred and many of those principles for which the reformers fought are now largely established. Others of their principles are still considered "radical" and reformers continue working toward their implementation. And there is no doubt that, within the Pullman strike as such, Carwardine was an extremely influential person. He has been overlooked in the writing of history, but he, among others, has played a large role in the shaping of that history which has ignored him.

There was a far reaching reaction to Carwardine's death. Editorials were written in many newspapers recognizing his lasting contributions. Sponsors of labor were rare in his day, pitifully rare, and it was a radical thing to oppose great moneyed interests. But when principle and policy clashed, there could be no choice with Carwardine. He believed in the cause of the strikers, so he fought for it. Wrath showered down upon him, from the interests he dared to challenge, from fellow ministers, and from many other sources. But the humanity of his appeal and its logic brought support and money. Newspapers began to follow him, funds were subscribed, and the public was aroused.

The editorial page of the *Chicago Herald and Examiner* for August 27, 1929, carried an article entitled, "He Was our Friend." It stated:

Dr. W. H. Carwardine, preacher, writer, fighter for the right, is dead, and this newspaper will not cease to miss his inspiration. Not that the other workers on the paper, the men and women who with daily gave to its service the best of their abilities, will ever forget him. But even his memory cannot make up for the loss of his presence. He was capable. He was widely experienced. He was deeply sympathetic. He was inevitably courageous, inevitably cheerful. For so many years he had walked with God that his counsel was that of a spiritual comrade. He was a veteran in goodness and sweet reasonableness. What he wrote had always about it something of the beauty of love. There are young men and young women who worked beside him by whom even the glory of religion will always be defined as having the Carwardine spirit. This afternoon he will be buried. But earth cannot hide, nor years obscure, the bravery of heart, the bright vigor of intelligence, the gaiety of courtesy, which he taught by his life even more remarkably than by his words. There was a man![22]

A co-worker with Carwardine at the *Herald and Examiner* office, Ashton Stevens, who wrote a weekly column concerning the theater, devoted a column to Carwardine and said, "I miss my old friend and colleague." He admired Carwardine for his applied Christianity, for being a clergyman who knew what the world was all about and saw that the church had a vital role to play in society, not apart from it. Religion was to make life more enjoyable, not to take the joy out of life. Stevens ended his column with the words: "He enjoyed a good play even more than I enjoyed a good sermon. He was a godly man who didn't know how to be miserable about it, and I miss his gusty, spontaneous laughter."[23]

The Rock River Annual Conference: Memoirs of Ministers and Ministers' Wives Deceased During Conference Year 1928 - 1929, had many good things to say about Carwardine. The style was extremely eulogistic, but made some good insights. It reminded its readers that the Pullman strike in the middle nineties occurred when it was not popular to espouse the cause of toiling classes by pen or voice. Carwardine espoused labor's cause in the face of a hesitant and unsympathetic press, when church leaders were timid, uncertain, skeptical and critical of his actions. In the field of journalism, he displayed the same courage with marvelous initiative. He gave evidence of the highest patriotism, the patriotism of humanity.

Often he seemed to be in advance of the policies of his day. He was characterized by a progressive temperament. His mind worked systematically, and he was truth in all its concatenations which helped to keep him poised and well balanced so that he never ran off on a tangent. He never lived on the siding; he always lived on the main track.[24]

An excellent analysis of Carwardine's lasting contributions was given in the *Chicago Daily News* on August 31, 1929, in reference to the remembrance of Labor Day. It stated:

> The active interest of religious bodies in industrial conditions and relations has grown apace as measured by the experience of one of their spokesmen. When the Rev. W. H. Carwardine was pastor of the Pullman church he undertook to understand why his parishioners and other fellow townsmen were on strike with the workers of the Pullman car shops. As he found out, he tried to make others understand, from his pulpit, in the newspapers and on the platform in many other cities. Then he was rebuked by many of his brethren in the ministry of his own and other churches. He was slighted in the appointments to the minor pastorates to which he was officially assigned. He was discredited by the press, especially in the religious weeklies. But he was the more beloved by his own people, their shopmates, and acclaimed by the labor unions as one minister who dared stand for social justice. Now when he is honored in death by church and city, Labor Sunday calls forth from very many pulpits the proclamation of the social gospel, from many religious weeklies articles and editorials on industrial rights and wrongs, and from the Federal Council of Protestant Churches, and from previous declarations of Roman Catholic and Jewish official bodies, programs for

pronouncement and action. Social service commissions are in the field to carry on this propaganda and carry out into action these programs to which their respective local, denominational, federated and interdenominational bodies have more or less committed themselves. Although all this rally to social justice was long delayed, although it is still more pronounced in word than in deed, although it falls short or down sometimes when put to the test, yet it marks a great change of front, a long march forward and direction that cannot be reversed. Critics of the churches who are impatient with their pace of progress should rate it by other slow changes made by such conservative bodies.[25]

Two letters might be referred to in closing, one written to Carwardine's wife upon his death, another written to Carwardine when he was alive and active. The Rev. Reese Bowman Kester followed Carwardine to the church in Greeley, Kansas, when Carwardine left for Illinois. He admired Carwardine's vital applied Christianity. Upon his death, he wrote a letter to Mrs. Carwardine. He said that when he moved to Greeley, he heard many good things about her husband, and thought he could never meet his standards. When he attended Garrett Biblical Institute and met him, he came to have even greater respect for him. He went on to say:

How many times have I reflected upon his Pullman experience; how far in advance he was in the social application of the Gospel when most of his brethren were cautious because they had not travelled that way before. He really was a pioneer in the application of the Gospel when for the most part our brethren were at best only academicians. Brother Carwardine was a brave far seeing man and his brethren came at length to understand his position as the champion of the larger rights of all men. He served the Church admirably in his position as religious editor of the *Examiner*. I loved him. I feel lonely now that he has gone into the heavenlies. If ever I am fortunate enough to enter that hill country of God I am sure that he will welcome me and help me to get acquainted with the new experiences.[26]

These words were, no doubt, very sincere words. However, Carwardine was a preacher also, and he was as aware as anyone that preachers tended to be eulogistic. There is another letter that he kept well preserved, which, considering his immersion in the Pullman strike and the pride he expressed so many times in being identified with the workers' cause, meant much to him. It was a letter written to him on July 23, 1894, in the midst of the strike. It came from the headquarters of the Central Strike Committee, and was signed by T. W. Heathcote, president; R. W. Brown, vice-president; and J. W. Jacobs, acting secretary. It will serve well in conclusion.

T. W. HEATHCOTE, Pres.   THEO. RODHE, Treas.   JNO. F. BERRY, Sec'y

Headquarters

168

CENTRAL STRIKE COMMITTEE,

TURNER HALL, KENSINGTON.

Address all Communications to JNO. F. BERRY, Sec'y Strike Committee, Box 551, Pullman.

KENSINGTON, ILL. _July 23d_ 1894

We do hereby assert and affirm that
R: W. H. Carwardine. is a man of sterling
ability. a clear thinker, an eloquent speaker.
Concise and to the point in his statements.
Having been a Resident of Pullman for a
Number of years, He is well known to the
People of Pullman and vicinity. The Rev-
is noted for his veracity and fearless devotion
to justice at all times.

He is respected by all and loved by
Many. We heartily indorse all that he
writes about the present strike
and the Town of Pullman. And can vouch
for the truth of the statements He makes.
Knowing full well that He is quoting facts
which He has personally ascertained to
to be true.

And will lay bare and unmask
the truth impartially and without
prejudice, 27

202

Address all Communications to JNO. P. BERRY, Sec'y Strike Committee, Box 551, Pullman.

KENSINGTON, ILL._____1894

As the Rev is clearly a disinteres[t?]
person Who residing here has been
made a circumstantial observer of the
cause and development of the present strike

        T. W. Heathcote   President
        R. W. Brown   Vice President
        J. W. Jacobs,   Act Secy

Well, how relevant is Carwardine's value system and social analysis to the 1980's and beyond? There are many indications that we may be living in the "Neo-Gilded Age." Just looking at a few of the many articles written in the 1980's is very telling: "The Great American Job Machine: The Proliferation of Low Wage Employment in the U.S. Economy," "The Declining Middle," "A Family Down and Out," "Reaganism is Harmful to Your Health," "Hunger in America: The Growing Epidemic," "Women and Children Last: The Plight of Poor Women in Affluent America," "Rich People, Poorer Country," "The Reagan Domestic Legacy: Greater Inequality and Destabilization," etc.

D. Stanley Eitzen and Maxine Baca Zinn are among many critics who cite situations such as:

> Reagan's consistent theme, packaged in images invoking God, flag, and country, is that the system is working...What he paints for us is a Norman Rockwell painting of America that omits its "dark side." The system is clearly not working for many people...The downside that Reagan clearly ignores includes:
>
> - Farmers are experiencing the worst depression since the Great Depression...
> - The number of individual and business bankruptcies, as well as bank failures, are higher than at any time since the Great Depression...
> - The federal debt...is sapping the treasury...
> - The National Coalition for the Homeless estimates that there may be as many as 3 million homeless (Associated Press. "Major Cities Report Increase in Homeless," Associated Press Release, December 18, 1986)...

- There are 32.5 million Americans - 1 out of 7 - who were living below the government's poverty line in 1987.

- The Physicians Task Force on Hunger in America estimates that some 20 million Americans are seriously hungry at least some period of time each month and that serious malnutrition impacts about 500,000 children. (1985:8-9)[28]

Eitzen and Zinn go on to build a case that the gap between the rich and poor has widened because of a shift in taxing and spending priorities. "Between 1977 and 1988 some $129 billion in income will have been shifted from the lower 90 percent of families to the top 10 percent." (Faux, Jeff. "The Party's Over, But Who Pays?" **The Nation**, January 30, 1988, p.128-130)[29]

As in Carwardine's era it is still unpopular to criticize the political, economic, social and religious status quo. Prophets are still unwelcome. Critics are still dismissed through name-calling and loaded labels.

So, how relevant is William Carwardine to the 1980's and beyond? The answer seems obvious, but that is a story for another day.

ENDNOTES

[1]"The Great Industrial Problem," *Evening Advocate* (Green Bay), March 26, 1897.

[2]*Ibid.*

[3]"Credit to Labor; Address by Rev. W. H. Carwardine of Chicago," *Kalamazoo Evening News*, September 8, 1896.

[4]"Says Future is Dark; Carwardine the Pullman Divine Talks of Labor," *Daily Northwestern* (Oshkosh, Wisconsin), September 6, 1897.

[5]"For the Cause of Labor," *Sioux City Journal*, March 31, 1898.

[6]*Ibid.*

[7]*Ibid.*

[8]*Ibid.*

[9]"Rev. William H. Carwardine, a Fearless Friend of the Firemen Who Has Done Much for the Twelve-Hour Day," *Chicago Fireman's Journal.*

[10]Campaign Headquarters, room 38, 92 LaSalle St., Chicago, campaign pamphlet for William H. Carwardine, Prohibition candidate for Illinois State Representative from the 27th Senatorial District, 1904.

[11]*Ibid.*

[12]*Chicago Fireman's Journal.*

[13]*Ibid.*

[14]A. W. Fairbanks, campaign manager for Carwardine's candidacy, 1904, for Illinois State Representative, circular letter on behalf of his candidacy, November 1, 1904.

[15]"He's Minister and Reporter, Too," *Register-Gazette* (Chicago), October 2, 1920.

[16]William H. Carwardine, "Reid's End, Our Duty," *Chicago Herald and Examiner*, January 22, 1923.

[17]William H. Carwardine, "When the Parents Fail," *Chicago Herald and Examiner*, February 13, 1923.

[18]*Ibid.*

[19]C. Zachus, instructor at Cooper Union for the Achievement of Science and Art, letter written to Carwardine after exam failure, June 7, 1875.

[20]Hampden Dougherty, letter written to Carwardine, May 22, 1879.

[21]*Greeley News* (Greeley, Kansas), September 4, 1886.

[22]"He Was Our Friend," editorial, *Chicago Herald and Examiner*, August 29, 1929.

[23]Ashton Stevens, "A Column or Less," *Chicago Herald and Examiner*, August 29, 1929.

[24]*Rock River Annual Conference: Memoirs of Ministers and Ministers' Wives Deceased During Conference Year 1928 - 1929* (Chicago: Methodist Episcopal Church, 1929).

206

[25]Graham Taylor, "The Nation's Labor Day Interests," *Chicago Daily News*, August 31, 1929.

[26]Reese Bowman Kester, letter written to Mrs. Carwardine upon the death of her husband, September 15, 1929.61.5

[27]T. W. Heathcote, R. W. Brown, and J. W. Jacobs, letter written to Carwardine from the Central Strike Committee on July 23, 1894.

[28]Stanley D. Eitzen and Maxine Baca Zinn, "The Reagan Domestic Legacy: Greater Inequality and Destabilization," Society's Problems: Sources and Consequences (Boston: Allyn and Bacon, 1989), p. 94-96.

[29]Ibid, p.96

BIBLIOGRAPHY

BOOKS

Baran, Paul and Sweezey, Paul M. *Monopoly Capital: An Essay on the American and Social Order*. New York: Monthly Review Press, 1974.

Bartlett, Irving H. *The American Mind in the Mid-Nineteenth Century*. New York: Thomas Y. Crowell Company, 1967.

Braverman, Harry. *Labor and Monopoly Capital: The Degradation of Work in the Twentieth Century*. New York: Monthly Review Press, 1974.

Beard, Charles and Beard, Mary. *The Rise of American Civilization*. 2nd ed. revised. New York: Macmillan, 1933.

Blum, John M., *et al. The National Experience: a History of the United States*. New York: Harcourt, Brace, and World, Inc., 1968.

Buder, Stanley. *Pullman: an Experiment in Industrial Order and Community Planning 1880 - 1930*. New York: Oxford University Press, 1967.

Carnegie, Andrew. *The Empire of Business*. revised edition. Westport, Connecticut: Greenwood Press, Inc., 1968.

Carwardine, William H. *The Pullman Strike*. Chicago: Charles H. Kerr and Co., 1894.

Clark, John Bates. *The Philosophy of Wealth*. 2nd edition. New York: Augustus M. Kelley, Publishers, 1887.

Cochran, Thomas and Miller, William. *The Age of Enterprise*. New York: Macmillan, 1942.

Cole, Donald B. *Handbook of American History*. New York: Harcourt, Brace and World, Inc., 1968.

Conwell, Russell H. *Acres of Diamonds*. New York: Harper and Brothers, 1890.

Curti, Merle. *The Growth of American Thought*. New York: Harper and Row Publishers, Inc., 1943.

Darrow, Clarence S. *The Story of My Life*. New York: Charles Scribner's Sons, 1932.

Davis, Allen F. and Woodman, Harold D. (eds.) *Conflict or Consensus*. Boston: D.C. Heath and Co., 1968.

Degler, Carl N. *The Age of the Economic Revolution 1876 - 1900*. Glenview, Illinois: Scott, Foresman and Co., 1967.

Dennis, Norman and Halsey, A. H. *English Ethical Socialism: Thomas More to R. H. Tawney.* ....Clarendon Press, 1988.

Dombrowski, James. *The Early Days of Christian Socialism in America*. New York: Octagon Books, Inc., 1966.

Doty, Mrs. Duane. *The Town of Pullman: its Growth with Brief Accounts of its Industries*. Pullman, Illinois: T. P. Struhsacker, 1893.

Dunne, Finley Peter. *Dissertaions by Mister Dooley*. New York: Harper and Brothers, 1906.

Eitzen, D. Stanley and Zinn, Maxine Baca. "The Reagan Domestic Legacy: Greater Inequality and Destabilization." in Eitzen, D. Stanley. *Society's Problems: Sources and Consequences*. Boston: Allyn and Bacon, 1989.

Gabriel, Henry. *The Course of American Democratic Thought*. New York: Ronald Press Company, 1940.

The Great Strike of 1894 and its Features: Organized Labor's Demands, as Formulated by President Debs, A.R.U., General Master Workman Sovereign, Governor Altgeld and the Federation of Labor; also the Opinions of the Press of the Country on the Late Strike and its Significance. New York: The Morning Advertiser, Publisher, July 20, 1894.

Harris, William H. and Judith S. Levey (eds.). *The New Columbia Encyclopedia*. New York: Columbia University Press, 1975.

Hays, Samuel P. *The Response to Industrialism*. Chicago: University of Chicago Press, 1957.

Hendrick, B.J. *The Life of Andrew Carnegie*. New York: Doubleday, Doran and Co., 1932.

Herron, George D. *The New Redemption* (New York, 1893).

Hicks, Granville. *The Great Tradition: an Interpretation of American Literature Since the Civil War*. revised edition. New York: Biblo and Tannen Booksellers and Publishers, Inc., 1935.

Hicks, John D. *The Populist Revolt: a History of the Farmers' Alliance and The People's Party*. revised edition. Lincoln: University of Nebraska Press, 1961.

Hofstatgdter, Richard. *The Age of Reform: from Bryan to F.D.R.* New York: Alfred A. Knopf, Inc., 1955.

Howard, Irving E. *The Moral Alternative to Socialism*. Chicago: Citizens Evaluation Institute, 1971.

Hubbard, Elbert. *A Message to Garcia and Other Essays*. revised edition. New York: Thomas Y. Crowell, Co., 1924.

Huberman, Leo. *We, the People*. revised edition. New York: Monthly Review Press, 1964.

Ionescu, Ghita. *The Political Thought of Saint-Simon*. London: Oxford University Press, 1976.

Jones, Peter d'A. *The Christian Socialist Revival 1877 - 1914*. Princeton, N.J.: Princeton University Press, 1976.

Josephson, Matthew. *The Robber Barons*. New York: Harcourt, Brace and World, Inc., 193 ? .

Keller, Albert G. and Davie, Maurice R. (eds.) *Essays of William Graham Sumner*. New Haven: Yale University Press, 1934.

Kennedy, Gail. (ed.) *Democracy and the Gospel of Wealth*. Boston: D.C. Heath and Co., 1967.

Kingsley, Charles. *Works*. London: 1887.

Kingsley, Charles. *Yeast*. Fourth Edition, London: 1859.

Koopman, H.R. *Pullman: the City of Brick*. Roseland, Illinois: Privately printed, 1893.

210

Lindsey, Almont. *The Pullman Strike: the Story of a Unique Experiment and of a Great Labor Upheaval.* Chicago: University of Chicago Press (Phoenix Books), 1967. (First published in 1942.)

Lukacs, George. *History and Class Consciousness.* Cambridge, Mass: MIT Press, 1922/1968.

Marcuse, Herbert. *An Essay on Liberation.* Boston: Beacon Press, 1969.

Marcuse, Herbert. *One Dimensional Man.* Boston: Beacon Press, 1964.

Marx, Karl. *Capital: A Critique of Political Economy.* Vol.1. New York: International Publisher, 1867/1967.

Marx, Karl and Engels, Frederick. *The German Ideology.* Part One. C. J. Arthur (ed). New York: International Publisher, 1845-46/1970.

Melville, Herman. *Moby - Dick.* Edited by Alfred Kazin. Boston: Houghton Mifflin Co., 1956. (First published in 1851)

McCloskey, Robert Green. *American Conservatism in the Age of Enterprise.* Cambridge: Harvard University Press, 1951.

Nugent, Walter T. K. *The Tolerant Populists: Kansas Populism and Nativism.* Chicago: University of Chicago Press, 1963.

Parrington, Vernon L. *Main Currents in American Thought.* New York: Harcourt, Brace, and Company, Inc., 1927.

Physician Task Force on Hunger in America. *Hunger in America: The Growing Epidemic.* Middletown, Conn: Wesleyan University Press, 1985.

Pollack, Norman. *The Populist Response to Industrial America.* Cambridge: Harvard University Press, 1962.

Poulantzas, Nicos. *Fascism and Dictatorship: The Third International and the Problem of Fascism.* London: NLB, 1974.

Raven, C.E. *Christian Socialism 1848 - 1854.* Fairfield, New Jersey: Augustus M. Kelley, Publishers, 1920. (reprint 1968)

Saint-Simon Henri. *1760 - 1825 Selected Writings on Science, Industry and Social Organizations*. (trans. and ed. by Keith Taylor). New York: Holmes and Meier Publishers, Inc., 1975.

Saint-Simon, Henri De. *Social Organization, the Science of Man and Other Writings*. (ed. and trans. by Felix Markham). New York: Harper and Row. (Harper Torchbooks), 1964.

Schlesinger, Arthur M., Jr. *The Age of Jackson* Boston: Little, Brown and Co., 1945.

Sidel, Ruth. *Women and Children Last: The Plight of Poor Women in Affluent America*. New York: Viking, 1988.

Smith, H. Shelton, Handy, Robert T., and Loetscher, Lefferts A. *American Christianity: an Historical Interpretation with Representative Documents*. Vol. II: 1820 - 1960. New York: Charles Scribner's Sons, 1963.

Stein, Leon. (ed.) *The Pullman Strike*. New York: Arno and the New York Times, 1969.

The Strike at Pullman: Published Statements of the Company Made During it Continuance. Pullman, Illinois: Privately printed, 1894.

Struik, Dirk J. (ed.) *The Economic and Philosophic Manuscripts of 1844*. New York: International Publishers, 1932/1964.

Sunseri, A. "The Military - Industrial Complex in Iowa." in B.F. Cooling (ed.) *War, Business, and American Society: Historical Perspectives on the Military - Industrial Complex*. Port Washington, N.Y.: Kennikot Press, 1977.

Swinton, John. *Striking for Life*. Privately printed, 1894.

Tawney, R. H. *Religion and the Rise of Capitalism*. New York: Mentor Books, The New American Library of World Literature, Inc., 1961. (First published in 1926: New York, Harcourt, Brace and Co., Inc.)

Veblen, Thorstein. *Absentee Ownership and Business Enterprise in Recent Times: the Case of America*. New York: Augustus H. Kelley, Publishers, 1923.

_____. *The Theory of Business Enterprise*. New York: Augustus M. Kelley, Publishers, 1904.

_____. *The Theory of the Leisure Class*. New York: Augustus M. Kelley, Publishers, 1899.

Ward, John William. *Andrew Jackson - Symbol for an Age*. New York: Oxford University Press (a Galaxy Book), 1962.

Warne, Colston E. (ed.) *The Pullman Boycott of 1894: the Problem of Federal Intervention*. Boston: D.C. Heath and Co., 1955.

Weber, Max. *The Protestant Ethic and the Spirit of Capitalism*. New York: Charles Scribner's Sons, 1958.

White, Alfred J. *Improved Dwellings for the Laboring Classes: the Need, and the Way to Meet It on Strict Commercial Principles*. Privately printed. 1879.

Whitman, Walt. *Democratic Vistgas, and Other Papers*. London: Walter Scott, 1888.

_____. *Leaves of Grass*. revised edition. New York: Avon Books, 1969.

Williams, William Appleman. *The Contours of American History*. Chicago: Quadrangle Books, 1966. (First published in 1961)

Yellowitz, Irwin. *The Position of the Worker in American Society 1865 - 1896*. Englewood Cliffs, New Jersey: Prentice-Hall, Inc., 1969.

ARTICLES, PERIODICALS, ASSOCIATION PAPERS

Alter, Jonathan et. al. "Homeless in America." *Newsweek*, (January 2, 1984), 20-29.

Associated Press. "Major Cities Report Increase in Homeless," Associated Press Release, (December 18, 1986.)

Ballard, Chester C. "The Rich Get Richer and the Poor Get Federal Budget Cutbacks," *Rural Sociological Society*, (1983).

Boskin, Michael J. "Reaganomics and the Poor: an Alternative Perspective," *Business Forum*, (Summer, 1982).

Broder, David S. "The State of the Union...as Reagan's Platform," *Des Moines Register*, (January 29, 1984), 2c.

Broder, David S. "Conservatism of Convenience - Let Smith Profit from Public Service," *Des Moines Register*, (May 20, 1982), 2a.

Brooklyn Eagle. September 29, 1880.

Bulletin (Muncie, Indiana). August 10, 1899.

Carnegie, Andrew. "Wealth," *North American Review*, (June, 1889), 653-664

Chachare, Bernadette P. "Reaganomics and the Black Poor," *Society for the Study of Social Problems*, (1982).

Chicago Daily News. 1894 - 1929.

Chicago Evening American. 1929.

Chicago Herald and Examiner. 1894 - 1929.

Chicago Inter-Ocean. 1894.

Chicago Journal. 1894.

Chicago Mail. 1894.

Chicago Record. 1894.

Chicago Times. 1894.

Chicago Tribune. 1894 - 1929.

Chicago Socialist, III, No. 36 (May, 1886), VII, No. 76 (Sept., 1889), VIII, No. 81 (Feb., 1890), London, England.

Chronicle, (San Francisco). September 16, 1894.

Clark, John Bates. "The Society of the Future," *The Independent*, LIII (July 18, 1901), 1649-1651.

Cobb, Stephen G. "Christian Socialism Now and Then: Carwardine and the Pullman Strike," *Midwest Sociological Society*, (1979).

Cohen, Jerry. "Timeless Town - a Restful Oasis in Wearying Waste," *Chicago Sun-Times*, Sec. 2 (September 24, 1961), 1-3.

Daily News-Tribune (Muscatine, Iowa). March 29, 1896.

Daily Northwestern (Oshkosh, Wisonsin). 1897.

Danziger, Sheldon. "Children in Poverty: The Truly Needy Who Fall Through the Safety Net," *Children and Youth Services Review*, (1982), 35-51.

Dispatch (St. Paul). August 25, 1894.

Dollars & Sense. "Reaganomics Report Card," *Dollars & Sense* No. 126 (May, 1987), 6-8.

"Drawing the Line," *Western Christian Advocate*, LXI (June 13, 1894). Cincinnati: Methodist Episcopal Church.

Ellen County Mirror (Ellen County, Texas). August 7, 1894.

Emerson, Stephen. "How U.S. Firms Lobbied for AWACS on Saudi Orders," *Des Moines Register*, (March 14, 1982), 1c.

Epstein, Samuel. "Perpetrating Myth the Getting of Cancer is Your Own Fault," *Des Moines Register*, (1981).

Evanston News-Index (Evanston, Illinois). August 26, 1929.

Evening Advocate (Green Bay, Wisconsin). March 26, 1897.

Faux, Jeff. "The Party's Over, But Who Pays?" *The Nation*. (January 30, 1988), 128-130.

Fishman, Walda Katz. "Reindustrialization: What Is It? Will It Work? and for Whom?" *Society for the Study of Social Problems*, (1981).

Friedland, Roger. "The Politics of Profit and the Geography of Growth," *Urban Affairs Quarterly*, (September, 1983), 41-54.

Galbraith, John Kenneth. "Shifting Costs from Richest (U.S.) to Poorest Governments (cities)," *Des Moines Register*, (February 18, 1982), 10a.

Ghent, W. J. "The Next Step: a Benevolent Feudalism," *The Independent*, LIV (April 3, 1902), 781-788.

Glazer, Nathan. "The Social Policy of the Reagan Administration: A Review," *The Public Interest*, (Spring, 1984), 76-98.

Globe Journal (Dubuque, Iowa). April 1, 1898.

Greeley News (Greeley, Kansas). Septebmer 4, 1886.

Guarasco, L. Richard and Peck, Gary. "The Political Economy of Brown Lung," *New York State Sociological Association*, (1983)

Harper's Weekly. "Revolutionary Statesmanship," *Harpers Weekly*, (November 24, 1894).

Harrison, Bennett; Tilly, Chris; Bluestone, Barry; "Wage Inequality Takes a Great U-Turn," *Challenge* 29 (March-April, 1986), 26-32.

Hour Week Journal of New York. August 5, 1882.
Huntley, Steve; Hilbreth, James H.; and Morse, Robert J. "Reagan's Revolution: Impact on Your Purse," *U.S. News & World Report*, (February 6, 1984), 20-23.

Huttman, John P. "Reaganomics and Employment Attrition," *Society for the Study of Social Problems*, (1982).

Jacklin, Thomas M. "The Civic Awakening: Social Christianity and the Usable Past," *Mid-America*, (1982).

Jirovec. Ronald L. "Reaganomics and Social Welfare: An Annotated Bibliography: Here's Help in Assessing the Impact on Programs, Clients, and Professionals," *Public Welfare*, (Fall, 1984), 23-27.

Journal (Providence). August 19, 1894.

Kalamazoo Evening News. September 8, 1896.

Kensington Advertiser (Kensington, Illinois). 1894.

King, William McGuire. "The Emergence of Social Gospel Radicalism: The Methodist Case," *Church History*, (December, 1981), 436-449.

Kingdom, The, VII - XI (Minneapolis, 1895 - 99)

Kopkind, Andrew. "The Age of Reaganism," *The Nation*, (November 3, 1984), 433; 448-51.

Kuttner, Bob. "The Declining Middle," *The Atlantic Monthly* 252 (July, 1983), 60-72.

Labor World (Duluth). February 3, 1900.

Lawrence, the Right Reverend William. "The Relation of Wealth to Morals," *World's Work*, (January, 1901), 286-292.

Lindsey, Almont. "Paternalism and the Pullman Strike," *The American Historical Review*. XLIV, No. 2 (January, 1939).

Marion Daily Chronicle (Marion, Indiana). May 1, 1899.

Marion News. May 2, 1899.

Martin, Keith D. "Reaganomics and the Poor: A Theological Perspective," *Church & Society*, (January/February, 1983), 10-20.

McCarthy, Coleman. "It May Be 'Moored in Morality,' But Capitalism Needs Repairs," *Des Moines Register*, (June 11, 1982.)

McGahey, Richard. "Calling Poor the 'Underclass' Only Obscures the Truth," *Des Moines Register*, (March 15, 1982), 1c.

McGrary, Mary. "The State of the Union...as Seen from Fantasyland," *Des Moines Register*, (January 29, 1984), 2c.

Mialon, Marie-France. "Reaganomics and Social Nonpolicy in the United States," *Revue Francaise des Affaires Sociales*, (January-March, 1983), 109-117.

Michalowski, Raymond. "The Politics of the Right," *Crime and Social Justice*, (Summer, 1981), 29-35.

Miller, Norman C. "How Rich Prosper at Expense of Poor in Reagan's Budget," *Des Moines Register*, (February 11, 1982.)

Navarro, Vicente. "The 1984 Election and the New Deal: An Alternative Interpretation," *Social Policy*, (Summer, 1985), 7-17.

New York Sun. December 9, 1883.

New York Tribune. July 7, 1894.

News (Galveston, Texas). August 26, 1894.

News Tribune (Detroit). August 19, 1894.

Newsweek. "A Family Down and Out," *Newsweek*, (January 12, 1987), 44-46.

Nicklason, Fred. "Henry George: Social Gospeller," *American Quarterly*, (1970), 649-664.

Northwestern Christian Advocate, XLII, Chicago: Methodist Episcopal Church, 1894.

Olsen, Andy. "Weapons Industry Business Booming," *The Daily Northwestern*, (1982).

Painter, Mary. "Poor Children: the Big Losers Under Reaganomics," *Food Monitor*, (July/August, 1982).

Pertschuk, Michael. "Reaganism is Harmful to Your Health," *The Nation*, (July 24-31, 1982):65, 83-84.

Pierce, Charles S. "Evolutionary Love," *The Monist*, III (January, 1893), 176-200.

Podesta, Anthony T. "People for the American Way," (non-mailing letter, January, 1984), 1424 16th St. N.W., Washington, D.C. 22036.

Pullman Journal. 1893 - 1894.

Pullman Review. 1893 - 1894.

"Reagan Going All Out for Big Business," *Multinational Monitor,* (January, 1983), 14,15.

"Reagan's Pressure Points," *The New Republic,* (August 29, 1983), 14,15.

Register-Gazette (Chicago). October 2, 1920.

Religious Philosophical Journal. September, 1894.

"The Report on the Chicago Strike," *The Nation* (November 22, 1894).

"Rev. William H. Carwardine, a Fearless Friend of the Firemen Who Has Done Much for the Twelve-Hour Day," *Chicago Fireman's Journal,* I (September 22, 1904).

Rock River Annual Conference: Memoirs of Ministers and Ministers' Wives Deceased During Conference Year 1928 - 1929. Chicago: Methodist Episcopal Church, 1929.

Sarri, Rosemary C. "Increasing Poverty through Structural Change: The Impact of the Reagan Cutbacks," *Society for the Study of Social Problems,* (1983).

Sioux City Journal. March 31, 1898.

Thompson, Susan Gotsch. "The Ideological Underpinnings of the Reagan Administration's Approach to Poverty," *Society for the Study of Social Problems,* (1985).

Toledo Bee. February 23, 1897.

Toledo Commercial. February 23, 1897.

Toledo Daily Blade. February 23, 1897.

Toledo Daily News. February 23, 1897.

Toledo Union. February 27, 1897.

Wallerstein, Immanuel. "The USA in Today's World," *Contemporary Marxism*, (Winter, 1981-82), 11-17.

Winnick, Andrew J. "Reagan's Economic Program and Supply-Side Economics: An Evaluation," *The Insurgent Sociologist*, (Summer-Fall, 1985), 23-38.

Wish, Harvey. "The Pullman Strike: a Study in Industrial Warfare, " *Journal of the Illinois State Historical Society*. XXXII (September, 1939), 288-312.

Yackley, Sol. "The Village that George Pullman Built," *Chicago Tribune Magazine*, (May 5, 1968), 82-895, 93, 95.

Young, T. R. "Class Warfare in the 80's and 90's: Reaganomics and Social Jusice," *Wisconsin Sociologist*, Spring-Summer, 1988), 68-75.

Zuckerman, Mortimer B. "Rich People, Poorer Country," *U.S. News & World Report*, (July 20, 1987):66.

REPORTS

Biennial Report of the Adjutant General of Illinois, 1893 - 1894. Springfield: State of Illinois, 1895.

Bluestone, Barry and Harrison, Bennett. "The Great American Job Machine: The Proliferation of Low Wage Employment in the U.S. Economy," a study prepared for the Joint Economic Committee, U.S. Congress, December, 1986.

United States Strike Commission Report on the Chicago Strike of June - July, 1894. Senate Executive Document No. 7. 53rd Congress, 3rd Session. Washington, D.C.: Government Printing Office, 1895.

OTHER SOURCES

Campaign Headquarters, room 38, 92 LaSalle St., Chicago. Campaign pamphlet for William H. Carwardine, Prohibition candidate for Illinois State Representative from the 27th Senatorial District, 1904.

Carwardine, William H. Address to graduating class of summer school, LaSalle, Illinois. June 24, 1896.

_____. "The Diary of a Voyage from England to the United States." September 26ff., 1871.

_____. Letter written to Mr. Peter Cooper, president of Cooper Union for the Advancement of Science and Art. May 31, 1875.

_____. Letters written to, and received from, Henry Demarest Lloyd, deposited with Wisconsin Historical Society, Henry Demarest Lloyd Correspondence - 1894-96, 1905-07, boxes 4,5,6,14.

Dougherty, J. Hampden. Letters written to Carwardine, May, 1879.

Evans, Nellie. Interview with author of dissertation, March, 1970. She attended Carwardine's church as a child.

Fairbanks, A. W. Campaign manager for Carwardine's candidacy, 1904, for Illinois State Representative. Circular letter on behalf of his candidacy, November 1, 1904.

Heathcote, T. W., Brown, R. W., and Jacobs, J. W. Letter written to Carwardine from the Central Strike Committee on July 23, 1894.

Jeffrey, R. Letter written to Rev. H. Harvey introducing Carwardine for ministerial study, September 15, 1877.

Kester, Reese Bowman. Letter written to Mrs. Carwardine upon the death of her husband, September 15, 1929.

Lloyd, Henry Demarest. Articles written for *Harper's Magazine*, but never published. Articles and galley sheets deposited in Wisconsin Historical Society, Lloyd Papers, box 36.

Zachus, J. C. Instructor at Cooper Union for the Advancement of Science and Art; letter written to Carwardine after exam failure, June 7, 1875.

INDEX